MW01534953

CODE : ADAM

the search for a lost generation is about to end

by

David Bryan

www.dbevangelist.com

Bloomington, IN   authorHOUSE®   Milton Keynes, UK

AuthorHouse™
1663 Liberty Drive, Suite 200
Bloomington, IN 47403
www.authorhouse.com
Phone: 1-800-839-8640

AuthorHouse™ UK Ltd.
500 Avebury Boulevard
Central Milton Keynes, MK9 2BE
www.authorhouse.co.uk
Phone: 08001974150

First published by AuthorHouse 9/11/2006

ISBN: 1-4259-4990-8 (e)
ISBN: 1-4259-4409-4 (sc)

Printed in the United States of America
Bloomington, Indiana

This book is printed on acid-free paper.

Cover Design by Doug Joseph

The author of this project has taken *author's prerogative* in capitalizing certain nouns and pronouns in Scripture that refer to the Church, the Bride, the Father, Son, Body, and other references to God and/or His people. Take note that the name satan and related names are not capitalized. The author has chosen not to acknowledge him, even to the point of violating grammatical rules. Unless otherwise indicated, Scripture quotations are taken from the King James Bible Version. When quoting Scripture the author at times adds **bold** or *italic* for emphasis

This project is dedicated to the many people who have inspired me with and imputed upon me the wisdom and knowledge of God. Whether through the power of prayer, personal ministry, or daily example, because of you, my life is changed forever and my heart cannot keep silent; the rocks will not cry out in my place!

Contents

PREFACE xi

INTRODUCTION
CODE - ADAM xiii

CHAPTER ONE
THE DAY THE SKY FELL 1

CHAPTER TWO
DO YOU HEAR WHAT I HEAR? 9

CHAPTER THREE
"WE'RE NOT IN KANSAS ANYMORE" 18

CHAPTER FOUR
UNFOUNDED FEARS 27

CHAPTER FIVE
A SUBPOENA FOR THE SAVIOR............................. 30

CHAPTER SIX
CODE ADAM (Where art thou?) 37

CHAPTER SEVEN
SLEEPING GIANTS 43

CHAPTER EIGHT
BEFORE THE ROCKS CRY OUT! 49

CHAPTER NINE
THE BEGINNING OF SORROWS 53

CHAPTER TEN
WHO'S YOUR DADDY? 56

CHAPTER ELEVEN
INSERT CHURCH HERE 60

CHAPTER TWELVE
THE SONS OF GOD..65

CHAPTER THIRTEEN
THE ULTIMATE GENERATION....................................70

CHAPTER FOURTEEN
IT'S OUR TURN!...77

CHAPTER FIFTEEN
A FINAL WORD..83

ENDNOTES 85

PREFACE

"The present generation has long awaited such a voice to speak into it. What we hold in our hand is not only a record of that voice, but the power to enter our times."

The Church world needs a "voice of challenge." In a recent documentary concerning a certain church denomination that has lost more than one and a half million constituents, a reporter approached a former member with a question as to why so many had departed their denomination. Her answer was surprising. She said, "My church asks nothing of me; I can do anything I want to do and they don't care ... so why do I need a church?" This precious lady left her church without a challenge and ultimately without a purpose! People of our time need more than a church to belong to; they need a challenge and a purpose! In the contents of this book, I am confident that you will find, as I have, that challenge often surfaces and purpose is clearly defined.

Meeting the author of this book was not an ordinary experience for me. He has made such an impression for a young man who has only been in the ministry a few short years. It was not difficult to see that he had talent, and it was growing at an exponential curve. It was not hard to see through his willingness, into the true force that was driving him. This made his calling quite evident. I found rather quickly that this was a young man driven by a purpose greater than him. Not only is David a young man with purpose, but **CODE ADAM** handles it well, also further defining where we are as a people of God, and where we should be! The content of this project plunges one into destiny that screams for an answer.

If you can be and if you will be challenged by the things of the Spirit, then dare to enter the place where the very heart cry of God can not only be heard, but demands to be responded to. If you are prone to revival, then you, too, will feel the urgency of this message. It's an unusual message that is sure to grab your interest from the start and hold it firmly until it is finally finished, and the voice comes alive within you like never before... "Adam, where are you?"

No moment is more right, and no people more important to the Lord than this. This project is not only the yearning of God's heart for His people, but the way home for those who have been lost from true usefulness. **CODE ADAM**... Make the contents of this book a priority for your spiritual man. It's a worthwhile investment that will bring great dividends.

Rev. William Sciscoe
Senior Pastor of The Church Triumphant
Columbus, Ohio

INTRODUCTION

CODE - ADAM

The search for the lost generation is about to end...

The hunger for absolute truth and abandonment to worldliness in our time has given way to some great manifestations of God's power in recent days. As the Lord appears on the scene, a fearful manifestation and a reverent and awesome reality has taken place. He is here, He is working among us as we have sought after Him to do, but where are we while He is working? The book **CODE ADAM** is a plea, a final urgent letter from God, speaking to the only people who can change our day — you and me! Thus says the Lord, "the fields are white, the harvest is ready, the hearts of men hunger, it's time to work... Where are you?"

THE THOUGHT THAT SPARKED IT ALL

July 27, 1981: Adam Walsh and his mom went shopping at the local mall. They parked the car where they always did. Holding hands, they crossed the parking lot and entered the north entrance (the same as always), having no idea that what lie just moments before them would change their world forever. The store entrance put them in the toy department. Right in the middle of the toys was the BIG ATTRACTION: a display of the latest video games, which was of particular interest to Adam. Several other children were playing with the game, so Adam asked if he could stay and play also. His mom said okay and told him to stay there until she returned from the lamp department.

The lamps were only about seventy-five feet away (out of sight, but not far). The lamps were out of stock, so Adam's mom left her name and number. She was gone only seven minutes. When she returned, Adam was not at the video game. His mother walked down several aisles, calling his name. She realized that not only was her son Adam gone, but all the children were gone, and the video game was silent. Adam's mom spotted a boy about Adam's age wearing the same hat as Adam. She asked the child if he had seen another boy with the same hat. He nodded yes and pointed to the west door.

Adam's mother was positive that Adam would not go out the west door, so she asked the toy department clerk, but she had not seen Adam either. Adam's mom began asking everyone she could find, but they all said the same things. "Oh, he probably just wandered off. I'll bet he's looking for you." "You know how kids are. Maybe he went off with the rest of the kids." Adam's mom insisted that he did not run off with the other kids, and that something was terribly wrong. All around her, clerks kept waiting on people, as if nothing had happened. She finally asked a clerk to page her son. "Adam Walsh, please meet your mother in the toy department."

Several more moments that seemed like eternity passed and still no response. After Mrs. Walsh went to her car twice to see if he was there, and looked for him on her own for two more hours, someone finally called the police department, but it was too late. Sixteen days later, his body was found and positively identified through dental records and a friend of the family.

Adam's abduction and murder sparked national attention and awareness. More than 150,000 fliers were printed and distributed in search of the six-year-old victim in the days following his abduction. This would not be the end of the story, however; in the days, weeks, and years that followed, Adam's name became synonymous with the search for missing children. It was this very case through which the "**CODE ADAM**" child safety program was created and promoted by the Wal-Mart retail stores, being named in memory of 6-year-old Adam Walsh. A multitude of other stores instituted the program as well; and on April 23, 2003 "The **CODE ADAM** Act" became law.[1]

The **CODE ADAM** act requires that the designated authority for a public building establish procedures for a child missing in any federal facility. The program is designed to train personnel and other public building authorities in strategies to not only prevent child abductions, but also to respond swiftly and efficiently in cases of suspected abductions on their premises.

When a "**CODE ADAM**" is in effect, a brief description of the child is obtained and provided to all designated personnel, who in turn stop their normal work to search for the child and monitor all exits. If the child is not found within ten minutes of initiating the search, the on-site personnel contact additional authorities with a "**CODE ADAM**."[2]

The recollection of this story or any like it, for that matter, will send chills through any parent's body. A "**CODE ADAM**" to a parent is like the sudden diagnosis of a terminal illness to a patient only expecting a routine exam at the doctor's office. A helpless urgency overwhelms as the mind begins to reel with confused emotion. Our hearts all bleed within us, and we draw those whom we have taken for granted near to our hearts and thank God we have them still with us.

My wife and I were recently in a store when a "**CODE ADAM**" went into effect. Being acquainted as I am with the subject matter, a whole new reverence and awe came upon me as I personally entered a completely different dimension than the one we were in. The only thing that I could think was that there was an all-seeing eye searching the hearts of men at that very moment, reminding me that it is time to move onward. "Here I am, Lord. Send me, I will go."

THE FIRST CASE SCENERIO

A similar case thousands of years before this one sparked the same urgency in a place called the Garden of Eden. A Father and his two children walked the Garden of paradise and perfection in the cool of the day; this was their routine. He hadn't been gone too long and had planned to meet them in their usual place when tragedy struck. When He arrived, it was immediately evident that something was horribly wrong...

"Adam, where art thou?" His urgent plea filled the air.

Frantically searching, the "eyes of God roamed the earth" (Zechariah 4:10) and the annals of time searching for the missing child. One prophet records the search as God: "looked *for this counter part* and He found none" (Ezekiel 22:30). This bond and relationship was so precious to God that not only did He span eternity and the universe in desperate search, but He eventually proved that He was even willing to die to mend its brokenness. You can imagine the pain that entered His heart when the objects of His affection were nowhere to be found.

No one seemed too concerned that this child was missing. All of creation seems to ignore the Father's urgency, unlike the day when Christ was crucified and the sky turned black, while the earth violently shook. The world seemed silent this day, but you can guarantee there was desperation in Heaven. The first alert was sounded and a "**CODE ADAM**" went out through the Garden, into all the earth, and down through the ages. "Adam, where art thou?"

The prize of God's possession, the one whom He had designed for fellowship and through which He would carry out His redemptive plan in the earth was missing! "Adam, where are you?" Yet the call goes further still...

In this, the culmination of time, God has prepared a generation that He has said would "shine like the brightness of the Heavens, a people who would lead many to righteousness" (Daniel 12:3), and stand as His mighty army in the earth. "Never has there been a generation like this," the prophet Joel proclaims. God has prepared them for the end of the age, and He would call for them when He was ready to complete His work in the earth.

I am glad to report that in recent days that call has come forth, and God has spoken very clearly concerning the time in which we now reside concerning the church. He had plans to meet right here but wait, something is horribly wrong... In many cases they are nowhere yet to be found! And so, the search is on...

"CODE ADAM" is a plea to our generation. Sinful mankind has been lost from the map of relationship and operation since the Garden of Eden, and when God has needed us the most we have proved that we have not always had the best attendance records. Sin, and the guilt and shame that accompany its potency, has done more damage to potential ministry than 1,000 years of persecution.

"CODE ADAM" is the distress signal of all ages, a signal to a generation that God has determined to use. This signal has gone out into the earth with such fierce intensity that "all of creation waits in eager expectation for the sons of God to be revealed" (Romans 8:19) NIV. Even the most beggarly elements of creation can sense the nearness of the appearing of these 'sons' on the scene of prophetic operation.

There are those of us whose spiritual ears have been set to the Master's frequency and have heard the signals and felt the grip of urgency. We have recognized that this is the point at which God has designated to meet with this His chosen generation, the "last Adam," if you please. But they are not here...

"CODE ADAM"! This is a desperate plea and a mass search in the earth here and now for the children of the Most High God. Generation X is no more. We must quickly find the missing, or in some cases, help them to find themselves. We must employ whatever means possible or necessary to locate them and help them to define who they are and what they are capable of, because God is going to need them soon!

hell has feared that someone would shed a little light in this direction, and it is about time that we did. We are living in times that require everyone to be involved; we cannot allow the enemy to abduct one more potential vessel; none can be lost! Of all generations, this is most important. Of all times, ours is most urgent. There are those among us this very hour that have been intimidated, wearied, beaten, and discouraged from action by the effects of sin and shame. But God has called us to apostolic action and authority like never before, and we must locate them and liberate them!

Hear the voice of God to our generation; "Now is the time, today is the day we must work while we have time, we must educate ourselves quickly. We must infiltrate every facet of society, and work the works that God has apportioned to us with power and authority, without fear or favor." **CODE ADAM**! It's time to move!

David Bryan

CHAPTER ONE

THE DAY THE SKY FELL

(September 11, 2001)

DISTRESS SIGNAL No.1
The birth of a new age

"No God no it can't be!" I ran to the radio on the shelf in my office to quickly find a station and tune in to find out what was going on, as soon as I got the phone call concerning what just happened in New York. I was up earlier than usual this morning; my soul had been troubled in me all night and I just couldn't seem to rest. I prayed until there was nothing left to pray for, and finally went to sleep. When I awoke, it was like the Lord and I just picked up where we had left off a few hours before. Today, some friends of mine would be leaving for the mission field, and I was scheduled to take them to the international airport around 9:00 AM.

"Maybe God was stirring my spirit to pray for them, interceding for some hidden danger that would lie ahead in their pathway?" I thought to myself. I just couldn't seem to put my finger on it. I felt no release from prayer or the presence of God, so I stayed near Him all morning and listened closely... Little did I know what was about to take place. It was 7:30 AM when I sat down at my desk to take a few notes. My mind raced, my heart was overwhelmed, and suddenly... an eerie moment of release; little did I know that we as a people were entering a dimension and time unlike any other before...

1

An hour had passed like a moment's time, so I got up and began to gather my things to head for the airport. It was just before 9:00 AM. The phone rang just as I was leaving; I was about to receive the news that would change our world forever...

An urgent voice on the other end of the line asked, "You haven't left yet?"

"No," I said, "but I am on my way out in just a few minutes."

"I think your plans may have changed!" the voice exclaimed. "You better call your friends and see if they've heard anything yet. There's been a hijacking in New York, and Washington D.C. and they are crashing planes into the government buildings."

I couldn't believe what I was hearing! I tuned in just in time to hear that all planes had been grounded and that our nation was on red alert. The next voices I heard were those of the reporters live on the scene in Manhattan, where the World Trade Center was beginning to come down. "People are jumping from the windows!" the news anchor's voice was broken with emotion; the sounds of sirens and the screams of a people in the background horrified beyond belief. This was all so surreal. I sat stunned in front of the radio for the next couple of hours.

I was overwhelmed, and in a moment of utter helplessness, I sank to the floor and wept. The world would never be the same. It was the end of an age of innocence and irresponsibility. It was all so surreal; we had always been told that such times were coming, but truth be known, we never really expected to see it unfold so dramatically in our day. I think maybe we were hoping God would rapture us before we had to witness such atrocities or take such personal account and responsibility for what we have believed in and preached for so long. I realize this date in history is a bit outmoded, but no one can truly grasp the gravity of what happened in our world this day. Stay tuned, there's more...

OUR INNOCENT EYES

We are the children of the "baby boomers." No one in our generation or time has truly understood the true cost of freedom in our land, not to mention the horrors of conflict itself. Our generation has been removed dangerously out of the way from feeling the true effects of reality on an international and even eternal level.

We were so far removed from truth and so severely desensitized to reality that our generation has become guilty only of fantasizing tragedy, as opposed to experiencing it firsthand. We look at the world around us as a virtual tour of reality, hoping to check out someday soon and go back to the way things were. In this generation, we stand just far enough away from reality not to feel the true effects of it, but not close enough to understand its true meaning and significance; our poor, innocent eyes.

On a recent trip to San Diego, my wife and I were privileged to tour the USS *Midway*, the first carrier commissioned after World War II. Before its decommission in 1992, this ship and those who have sailed on it have seen a lot of history; from the surrender of Japan at the end of WW II to the Gulf War in 1991. Our guide for much of our tour on this particular day was a man by the name of Vern. Vern, now a retired navy man, was the air boss (or as they would call him, the '*UTMOST*') from 1973-1975. From the fifteen-by-fifteen-foot eagle's nest (or control tower) the air department officer (or Air Boss) and assistant air department officer (also known as the Mini Boss) oversee events on the deck below. The Air Boss watches recoveries and the aft portion of the flight deck while the Mini Boss looks forward to the launch. The Air Boss is responsible for the safe launch and recovery of aircraft, elevator runs, aircraft movement on the flight deck, and arresting gear.

It was in this very position on April 29, 1975 that Vern witnessed the end of the Vietnam conflict as the USS *Midway* became an island to thousands of Vietnamese refugees. One incident in particular that will forever be etched in the halls of history was that of a Vietnamese major who landed a two-man plane on the deck of this old vessel. This two-man plane, it turns out, was carrying the major, his wife, and five children, who live in freedom today here in the United States because of these courageous men and their ability to work and think fast.

Hearing Vern tell of his personal involvement on this particular day in history, I thought to myself, "What a moment to witness!" But Vern not only witnessed it, he was involved in the successful execution of this very risky maneuver. I had read a bit about this particular incident and so I was familiar with some of things that transpired on this day in history, but what an honor it was to meet the man who helped to carry it out, and to sit in the very seat where this man helped to make history. I watched Vern as he told his story with such fervor and pride. My own heart welled up within me as he talked. Then I looked around at those who were with me in the eagle's nest overlooking the flight deck. Most of them were younger and seemed detached and uninterested... Because they weren't there, this was something far beyond their ability to comprehend.

It was a sad but true reality. In our time, people of our generation make movies about things like this, but times like these cast a fresh realization upon us that we cannot deny.

Could it be that our willful ignorance and temporal, secular, materialistic innocence has removed us from being able to comprehend the times in which we now live? I fear so, and I am afraid that if we do not awaken to our day while it is day that we will sleep on into the night... "O watchman, what of the night?"[1]

THIS IS NOT A TEST!

Weeks after this day of infamy, my mind (and a million others I'm sure) ran wild with thought. The innocent eyes of our time were now dimmed, not only by what this act of terror had brought us, but by the horrors of a greater reality than this... There would be more to come; this is only the beginning. Not necessarily more terrorism, or war, but something.

This is not a test, this is the real thing. Smoke filled the skyline of New York City and Washington D.C. today, but by evening, strangely enough, even in the town where I lived at the time, it seemed to fill even the skyline there as well... Reality was closing in fast. Everything I looked at or heard for days and weeks thereafter seemed to connect to this day. A child laughing, a dog barking, an airplane overhead; the innocent sounds of everyday activity turned somehow to a very harsh reminder that God was trying to get our attention through all this.

The laughter of a child became the sobs of now fatherless children. The barking dogs became the search-and-rescue workers sifting through tons of wreckage for signs of human life or remains. The sound of a jet overhead became an airliner without a pilot plunging violently to the earth. The sky was falling, reality was quickly closing in upon us, and life would never be the same.

I kept thinking, "Couldn't we have gone about this a different way, Lord? What else has to happen before we wake up?" Like treading the valley of a crumbling mountain, we were closed in on every side, and there's no way out, and no way to turn back. What a humbling, helpless feeling. We cannot turn away, this is not a test, and everything that we have ever known or been taught will be required of us now.

The time spoken of by so many of our forefathers is upon us. We heard them screaming for years, "It's coming, it's coming, be ready, be instant, be in season. God is going to do some things in the earth before His return that will cause many to see and know." And now, that time is upon us, and we are forced to awaken to it. Have we done enough? Are we ready? Reality quickly sets in, and the real facts are that a few plaques in an office across town are not going to get the job done. It is our turn to step onto the scene and God is ready to use more than just pretty faces and convoluted verbiage.

If today had begun the thirty-day countdown to the end of the age, who among us would stand ready to carry on the message to the end without fear or favor? Who among us is there now?

Oh how our hearts did bleed this day, and our minds ran wild with thought. I couldn't help wonder what was going on in the mind of God...

FOREVER CHANGED

What can we say but that from this moment on, we are forever changed? We will never see things the way we had before this time. Human history and understanding has reached its extremities. A generation was born overnight. It is the dawning of a new day.

Many people are not truly aware of what really happened on the morning of September 11, 2001 not only in this country, but in the earth. This was not just a security breach; it was a supernatural manifestation of the powers of the age of the anti-Christ flexing themselves in the earth. Demonic forces were dispatched via the airwaves in an instant; these powers were sent to destroy and tear down not only a nation but also a people...

If Heaven didn't have our attention before this, hell sure had it now. These were the manifest powers of one who "knows he has but a short time" and fears not to be as bold and as audacious as necessary unto the very end. You may remember the reports of people wandering aimlessly through the streets for days, nowhere to run, nowhere to turn, nowhere to lay their troubles. The world on the outside of the walls of this great church will live on with the memories and the horrors that have unfolded around them. But for us, the chosen and the called, this day is more than a reminder; it is a reality check, a wake-up call. A literal warning to us as a people that we no longer be ignorant of our times, or slothful in responding to the desperate needs of a dying world around us.

Everything that we had ever thought changed in an instant. In the "land of the free and the home of the brave," we had became instant prisoners, prisoners of fear, prisoners of doubt, and prisoners of the times in which we were created to be free to operate. For so long, it seemed that things were moving along so well. We thought we had everything figured out and under control. The real facts were, however, that our society was out of control and fading fast. Our foundations were crumbling beneath our feet in both the secular and the church world.

The facts are, we have done too well in the most dangerous areas of existence here in America, and not well at all where it matters most. Everything was fine in our little world, so we said. We have our preachers, we have our doctrines, we have our counselors, and our board of directors, and while we're at it "we have all the food and money we need too..." (Revelation 3:17).[2]

The danger of such narrow vision, whether it be in the church or secular world, is that such one-sided thinking can only hold a people for so long in a world of constant motion and change that demands to be lived in, and a clock that stops for no one. We become archaic and useless in an instant, powerless to face the age! And that's exactly what happened on this day.

Suddenly our SUVs and our designer suits become very insignificant in comparison to the greatness that lies before us. Something bigger than us had finally come upon us, and what's more, something even bigger is on its way. It was the fire drill for God's great day of judgment, and we were weighed in the balance and found wanting.

In just a few hours one Tuesday, it had become very apparent that all of our social and religious bandages only hid what has needed to be addressed all along. None of us wanted to admit that we were not living up to our potential. But the truth of the matter is, though our speech was at times very large, our actions paled in comparison.

Notice that in the days immediately following the national tragedy of September 11, every branch of government, federal and local, great and small, began to realize just how unprepared they were for times of such magnitude. Emergency crews and major city management crews were finding that they were not prepared physically or financially for something that they knew all along was destined to happen. This is a signal to the church of the Living God, it was time to mobilize, time to enact all that we have stood for; this is not a test. We are that generation!

This takes on a completely new meaning in the hearts of those of us who truly call ourselves Christians, and I pray it will for all who are hearing the great clarion call. This was our day of awakening church, and the words have never rang so clearly: "Be ready always to give an answer to every man that asks you a reason of the hope that is in you with meekness and fear" (1 Peter 3:15).

Again we hear Jesus say, "Be ready, because in such an hour as you think not, the Son of man comes..." I understand now the cry of the people recorded by John the revelator when they said, "[please] let the mountains fall on us, hide us from the face of Him that sits upon the throne... for the day of His wrath is come; and who shall be able to stand?" (Revelation 6:15-17). There's nowhere to hide, no one else to blame. The great and mighty will dwell with the poor and lowly on the same plane of desperation; not all the money and notoriety in the world will change this ultimate moment of reality. "Who can stand?" Truly, we are changed forever.

CHAPTER TWO

DO YOU HEAR WHAT I HEAR?

(Tuning our ears to hear the voice of the Master)

Just as there are distinct voices and dialects of tongue, there are certain sounds for certain seasons and situations in life.[1] The sound of laughter for joy, the screams of horror for fear, the gasp and sigh of hope, and the wail and groan of utter despair. Any good listener should be able to discern the sound, right? We would all like to think so, but are we truly tuned to hear the Master's call?

In recent years, a certain sound has been coming forth, but it has been silenced by the noise of our own selfishness and busyness! A cry for hope, a cry for healing, a cry for love, and a cry for truth; but we were all too busy in our own world, building our own kingdoms, planting our own gardens, and living in our own little dream homes to hear. In comparison to our big plans, it was very unnoticeable.

We didn't hear the voice when thousands of immoralists marched in Washington,[2] so now we are fighting them in our public schools and even our churches. We wouldn't hear its low, soft tones just beneath the lyrics of the musical messages that have now successfully warped our children's minds into thinking that all good is against them, so now we are desperately fighting to keep them under the protection of the God-given authority of their parents.

We didn't hear the cry in Waco, Texas on April 19, 1993 when 100 innocent people died because of a doctrine and religion that even those who perished never really understood.[3] We didn't hear the cry from Oklahoma City on April 19, 1995 when 168 innocent lives were destroyed,[4] neither did we hear it during the Columbine High School massacre of April 20, 1999. No, we didn't hear the cry because our ears have been deafened to one of the most important sounds this generation could ever hear: a cry for help and hope. It wasn't the voice of a dying world alone that we should have been hearing, but it was the voice speaking one spiritual frequency lower than this; the voice of God desperately trying to get the churches' attention.

Our spiritual senses seemed to have been warped and our ears too heavy to hear the cry. As of late, however, there seems to be a tuning in. God's voice is not as mysterious as we have led ourselves to believe. The supposed mystery is that God speaks, yet He speaks in another dimension, a dimension that cannot be casually entered into. It's time for us to reckon with what His voice is saying, and heed the cry.

"Behold, I stand at the door, and knock: if any man hear my voice, and open the door, I will come in to him, and will sup with him, and he with me... He that has an ear let him hear what the Spirit says unto the churches" (Revelation 3:20-22).

When reality finally breaks through upon those of us who "know" and understand that God has been speaking to us, desperately trying to get our attention, it won't take long to sense the urgency of the moment in which we dwell. Even as I write these words, my mind shakes with violent turbulence; "It's time, it's time, let's lean in closely and hear what the Master says!"

THE VOICE OF GOD

"When the Savoir calls I will answer, when He calls for me I will hear Him. When the Savior calls I will answer, I'll be somewhere listening for my name."[4] The words of the old hymn so innocently sung so many years ago. But are we really tuned in? The hour in

which we now reside demands that we listen more intently than ever for the voice of our Lord, lest we miss the final call...

"All right, Lord, you've got my attention; what would you like?"

I used to feel sorry for men like Jonah until I realized that God was desperately trying to speak to him and into his generation. Most of us know the story, so I do not need to go into great detail here, only to recapitulate the dramatic turn of events that others had to go through because Jonah would not heed the voice of God. You know it is very sad and even amazing what people will allow themselves to go through before they will actually stop and heed the voice of God! There are those ever-famous cases and countless testimonies of those who have been taken right to death's door before they will finally tune in.

A minister once related to me his story of how he came into the ministry... He carried his calling for quite some time evidently, but he would not acknowledge it. After losing one child tragically, he came down with some strange illness that could not be treated and was lying on his deathbed ignoring the voice that grew stronger from day to day. Unknown to him, his wife had tuned her ear to the voice of God for quite some time, and she knew that God had called her husband to preach and that He had been speaking to him for quite some time.

Her husband never shared with her the call upon his life, until one day while on his deathbed his wife, emboldened with fury, said to him, "When are you going to listen to God?" Needless to say, he finally answered the call!

I know what you're thinking; I thought the same thing: "What a rough way to go," but the truth of the matter is that many go the way of tribulation before they will actually learn to hear and obey the Master's voice. Have you ever wondered why it is that we only learn the hard way these days?

There seems to be a common thread of evidence within the lives of those who seem to have learned the hard way. It appears that this one hidden thread greatly contributes to spiritual deafness, which in turn keeps one from receiving the instruction needed to enter into the greater dimensions of God. The common thread is this: we cannot HEAR whom we do not FEAR.

Think about it; if some pipsqueak came to you and said, "Give me your lunch or I'll stomp on your foot," your response would be quite obvious. Maybe a giggle or two before the hammer of judgment fell, and finally you might say something like "Get lost," or "Try it and see what happens." Very few people that I know would give in to such a demand. But when someone bigger than you, who has the power not only to take your lunch, but possibly even your life, approaches with the same demands, your response would be drastically different, without doubt.

It is sad to say, but in the eyes of so many today, God has been made to look small and secondary to all else, thus His voice becomes like the voice of the little pipsqueak saying "Give me your heart." And out of ignorance, and self-will we respond, "Get lost; who do you think you are?" *They will not hear Him whom they do not fear.* Don't ever forget this.

We live in the generation that sports the "NO FEAR" attitude. We have allowed our peers and kindred to fall under the spell of entertainers and teachers whom we call role models, who have taught them to fear nothing; not life, not death, not authority, and not God. Countless numbers in our time have walked far beyond boundaries set by the Word of God for our protection, without truly considering the consequences, simply because they have not truly learned to fear the Lord.

A LITTLE LOUDER, YOU SAY?

Yes, I am talking to you! Even in the church world, it has been very hard to hear the voice of God. Why, you ask? Because most of our absolutes have been squandered by men who prefer to propagate their personal agenda and ideologies, rather than speak the truth of God and face reality, no matter what the repercussion. These have silenced the voice of God for too long; providing a place for the unrepentant and rebellious to hide. God is not about helping the sinner to find new places to hide, but rather new places to dwell for the pure in heart.

Politics and propaganda have provided too many places in the church world for people to hide out, as opposed to being found and fixed. Too many have been lost, because as long as they will vote for or support the movements and kingdoms of men, then the rulers of these kingdoms provide places for the unrepentant to hide, and thus the voice of God is silenced.

Louder yet, you say? ABSOLUTES ARE NOT FOR SALE!!! "Buy the truth and sell it not!" (Proverbs 23:23). Opinions are the only thing purchasable, and they are subject to change at any moment, so be careful who you get yours from (it will not retain its value). "Here is the beginning of all wisdom, FEAR GOD and keep His commandments." It gets no plainer than this. The one is contingent upon the other. We could actually even say that the "fear of God is the power to keep the commandments."

We have, through neglect and ignorance, not taught ourselves or our children to fear the Lord; in turn, they cannot hear Him. Are you ready for this? We leave the service and joke about the message and even the messenger, and expect to hear the voice of God for ourselves?! We have even sometimes dismissed that God could have been there altogether, because of the vessel He may have spoken through. We have missed it for far too long, and it is sad to say, but it has destroyed not only the power of truth in our times, but our ability to truly hear.

We call ourselves Christians and argue with the church across town over issues that cannot even be supported by the Word of God. We spend more time and effort on issues that come from our own insecurities than we do with Truths that come from the Throne of God. God help us all. There is not a famine of preachers, nor of bread or money, but of "hearing the Word of God" (Amos 8:11).

"THE VOICE OF GOD IS SILENCED FIRST BY MEN WHO REFUSE TO SPEAK THE TRUTH, AND SECONDLY BY OTHERS WHO REFUSE TO HEAR AND OBEY." – **D. Bryan**

WHAT'S IT GOING TO TAKE?

That's a fearful thought, what is it going to take for some to hear? As aforementioned, all too often, God has to use the dramatic and even the catastrophic to prove a point and get our attention. I wonder what people were thinking in Noah's day, watching this crazy old man build a boat out in the middle of a desert?

Noah doesn't seem to have minded what other people were thinking; he seemed to be confident with the fact that he had heard from God and he just went about to complete his task. The world around him, however, mocked and laughed at even the possibility that God could have spoken such things to such a man.

Sadly the people of Noah's day were all too busy to hear what God was saying. "No thanks, I've got my own beliefs, Noah." They continued about their regular routine, when suddenly, something strange started happening. Water started falling from the sky, one drop, two, three, and all of a sudden, the heavens poured with rain. God had spoken, and they didn't listen, and now it was too late. They were in trouble and they knew it. They ran to the ark, but God had already shut the door!

God had been speaking to them through Noah for quite some time, but they had no fear or respect for the man Noah or the God he served. They did not fear, and so they did not hear, until it was entirely too late. It must have been a horrible sound to be shut in the ark of safety, hearing the screams of terror as those who refused to listen tried to climb and claw their way to safety. Then the waters grew silent as a whole generation was washed away.

The Apostle Paul went so far as to say that the Spirit "speaks expressly" in the later times. Simply meaning that He has gone to great pains to make sure that He can be clearly understood, and all who are in tune will hear what the Spirit is saying, and will be spared a horrible ending. Remember, God hides nothing He intends to do from His servants. "He that has an ear let him hear..." (Revelation 2:7).

TUNING IN

God gave Moses Ten Commandments as the basis of a religious, moral, ethical, and social law. There was, however, one precursor to the law that must first be fulfilled before any true instruction could be given, or even properly followed. "**HEAR,** O Israel." "Observe and do the things that I say." God was trying to tune the ears of all of Israel to hear His voice, because there were many things that He would have to say in the days, weeks, and years to come, and He knew that they would not be able to receive them if they were not tuned in.

Jesus said to His disciples before their ears were tuned to the Spirit, "I have many things to say to you, but you cannot bear [or understand] them now..." Jesus knew it would take a spiritual tuning of the ears to be able to truly hear His voice.

We hear Him say repeatedly to the New Testament church, "He that has an ear, let him hear what the Spirit is saying to the churches." Herein is a great understanding... The voice that is speaking to the church is a spiritual voice; therefore, we MUST be in the spirit to be able to decipher its message! "HEAR O CHURCH!!!" Too many are simply not listening to the voice of God, and are not tuned to the frequency of the Spirit. Jesus said again, "My sheep KNOW MY VOICE..." And furthermore, they HEED it! "My words are SPIRIT and they are life."

Herein is the difference between religion and relationship. Those who know Him hear and obey... 'Hearing is believing,' and believing is doing.

In a day and time when it has become more popular to simply go through the motions than actually live out the message, we need a fresh tuning to the Word of God. James says, **"Don't just listen to the Word, and deceive yourself by not obeying its commands; DO WHAT IT SAYS. Anyone who listens (or claims to have listened) to the Word of God, but does not actually do what it says, is like a man who looks into the mirror at himself, turns away and immediately forgets what he looks like"** (James 1:22-24 NIV; additions mine).

James's description is of a man who has had a very shallow and temporary experience that lasts only as long as he stands in front of his mirror. The time in which we live prophetically is often referred to and compared to as Laodecian church age by virtue of similar characteristics. It was the Laodecian church that was quoted as saying, "We have all we need, we can take care of ourselves." Interestingly enough, the only thing required of this age is the ability to hear.

"Behold I stand at the door and knock: if any man HEAR MY VOICE, and open the door, I will come in to him, and sup with him, and he with me" (Revelation 3:20). Other ages and churches before this were required to "repent," "return," "remember," "be watchful," and "strengthen the things which remain." But to our age, it is simply stated: "HEAR."

Hear: The voice of God speaking into a valley of bones dried by years of formalism and redundant religious motion; The bones of a generation dried by the winds of time gone by, and to this generation of sleeping giants, the voice of God speaks, "Oh ye dry bones, <u>HEAR</u> THE WORD OF THE LORD!" (Ezekiel 37:3,4).

Paul says, "The Spirit speaks expressly [or specifically, even urgently] that in the later times, some would depart from the faith..." But notice here that Paul is referring to what the Spirit is speaking and preparing the church for and not what he himself would say. "HEAR O ISRAEL!" Whether Paul was the author, or Johnny Nobody, the message was for a certain time, and the Spirit of God spoke it specifically. We do well to heed it. Who said it isn't the focus here; who hears it is. The message was a warning concerning our age. We will be spared much confusion and grief just learning to tune in.

This is a lesson we could learn well in our day: No matter what shape or form the message may come in, we must learn to hear God's voice. One minister once told me, "Young man, you'll go far when you can learn to hear the voice of God in any situation." The hearing ear profits most of all. We must turn our eyes from humanity alone, and learn that God's voice has many mouthpieces and His letters many pens.

In the beginning of time, God met and communed with Adam and his wife through a gentle breeze "in the cool of the day" if you please. In the book of Numbers 22:27-28, the Lord's voice spoke through the mouth of a mule! Again the Bible says that the **"rooster crowed and Peter remembered the words of Jesus... and he went out and wept bitterly" (Matthew 26:74, 75).**

Yes, you read it right. A rooster crowed, and Peter was convicted and brought to an altar of repentance. A rooster was used to help the great apostle to "remember the words of JESUS!" In the story of the young man Samuel, while staying at the temple with the priest Eli, the Bible reveals that God spoke to the young man in the middle of the night. Each time the voice of the Lord called unto him, however, something interesting was happening. Samuel heard only the voice of Eli the priest (1 Samuel 3:1-11).

The voice of God sounded like the man of God. In the same manner, God is speaking today. We have some of the greatest vocal conduits ever: preachers, teachers, prophets, apostles, evangelists, tongues, interpretations, situations, vocalizations, and a host of other means; we are without excuse! We must tune to hear the voice and instruction of God through them. We must know that it is He that speaks and none other.

CHAPTER THREE

"WE'RE NOT IN KANSAS ANYMORE"

These are the ever-famous words of the innocent little girl Dorothy in *The Wizard of Oz* in response to the fact that she and her dog Toto were swept by a great wind into a land completely unfamiliar to them. It is an interesting correlation here because modern-day American Pentecostalism has its roots in Kansas as well, Topeka to be exact. It was Topeka, Kansas in the early part of the last century where a group of young Bible students gathered under the direction of a man named Charles Fox Parham. These earnest seekers of the true apostle-like experience became pillars of the Pentecostal experience in America today. We sure have come a long way since those earnest and innocent days of pursuit; now the dark clouds of time have gathered to spawn a whirlwind of change that has carried our present generation far from what we would call familiar. We too can truly say that we are not in Kansas anymore!

A lot of time has passed since those first great and glorious days of awakening here in America. The things that once helped to initiate the work of God in our country have now become a great part of the foundation of what we are experiencing in these times, and yet there remains a work to be completed. Time has so quickly passed and the world around us now beats to the rhythm of a completely different drum. It is a fearful realization, but instead of pressing forward in many areas of operation, we seem to be falling farther and farther from the simple things that once defined and empowered us.

18

There was a certain zeal and fearlessness about these modern pioneers, a progressive determination that no matter what anyone thought or said, they were going onward. Where is that same bold spirit now? It's not time to stop and set up camp yet; we're not in Canaan! In many ways, we have set up camp and we're trying to operate in this time with tools that have either been antiquated or are extinct. There is no way that we should expect to approach the times that are now upon us in the ways that our fathers did and be successful on the same level as they were. God is progressive and He created a world to grow and be progressive also. We must learn to think on a much broader scale in a much broader time. "Greater things than these shall you do." The devices that once worked so well in times past are totally foreign and obsolete to our age. We are not in Kansas anymore! We must step up to meet our times and operate within them, as those who have gone before us have done.

We do not need 100 reasons why Jesus could return soon, but I can think of at least 100 and a few more why we had better be ready when He gets here! We must step up to our times.

Our generation is unlike any other before it, in that history alone can no longer be our guide. The great pioneers who have brought us this far have been called one by one to rest from their labors, therefore, we can no longer depend upon that which was intended to be foundational to our times to do anything more than be foundational. It's time to build upon what these men have left unto us and not again, we are but "standing on the shoulders of these giants."

There has been a certain turning of the tides in recent days. Our intelligence has taken us as far as we can go in the modern world. Our money and our prosperity have proven to be quite insufficient in light of the reality that lies before us. This is not only the culmination of an era, but it is the culmination of all ages, and as we have previously established, nothing will ever be the same. It may come as a great shock for us to hear God say, "All right, folks, it's My turn now, you've gone as far as you can go." In one stroke of Divine motion, the world has changed; out with the old and in with the new. So many things that were so commonplace among us just a few short years ago, are now uncomfortably out of place and yet we are called to move on.

As the great voices of our past fall silent, there is a hope; there is a generation among us that God is preparing during this time of transition and ultimate change. This generation will bring fresh voice and vision, even new meaning to the times in which we live. To this generation, let it be known that we must understand that the foundations can NEVER MOVE (these stand sure), but the materials with which we build upon them must be flexible enough to withstand the winds of our age.

The world around us has gone through some very dramatic changes in recent years. These changes have greatly affected our vision and direction as the people of God, whether or not we care to admit it. Thus, we must be ever cautious and careful. God knew that no one else would be able to handle the times in which we live. Thus, He concealed much of the information concerning these times from those who have gone before us, lest they try to work a work in a time that had not yet been prepared to receive it. (Note: There are those in past times who have tried to do so and were greatly misunderstood.) I believe that God allowed Daniel to see everything he wrote about and a whole lot more in his prophecy. But God told Daniel specifically, "Shut up the book, seal it until the end time" (Daniel 12:4). God has kept men from knowing the times, to protect them from destruction as well as from confusing His purpose.

Men would like to think that somehow we are in a 100-year cycle of history and that the things we are witnessing in our time are all common occurrences. The hope is and the talk on the street is that things will return to "normal" (whatever that is). In some small ways, this may ring true, but the sobering facts are that in many more ways, things will never be the same. We're not in Kansas anymore, folks.

Those who have gone before us conquered their time; this is how they made history. They have given us hope and aspiration for the days that lie ahead. They conquered their day, now we must conquer ours... No one else can do it for us.

THE SECONDHAND GENERATION

I don't know about you, but as a child, whenever I was given something that belonged to someone else, I felt cheated. There was never a real sense of respect or belonging for whatever the object may have been; it was just a hand-me-down, worn out, left over, and overused. To say the least, it was not respected because it wasn't truly mine. I remember when I was a boy, all I wanted for Christmas one year was a brand-new pair of hockey skates. Everyone else was getting some sort of new invention or creation, but all I wanted was a nice shiny new pair of hockey skates, just like the real guys used. Instead, all I received was a pair of worn out skates that a friend of the family had outgrown. I'm not complaining these years later; my parents did the best they could, but the skates weren't mine, and I never really appreciated them. From what I recall, they didn't last very long.

There is, however, always an excitement about the new. No one else has touched it but me. I am the first! What a sense of pride and ownership. What a keen, fresh sense of possession, responsibility, and accomplishment.

We need a fresh "baptism" in our times, if you will, of personal ownership and responsibility when it comes to the things of God. Our generation has lived too long from the "hand downs" of a time that we cannot even relate to, socially or spiritually. Think about it — we live in a generation of uneducated voters, and victims of crimes not even done in our time! Our generation is voting, but they're not sure who or what for. They are crying and they're not sure why. They're running but they're not sure what from! Our forefathers' purpose has deteriorated into mere formalism and protocol. We have lived too long from another generation's experience, and in the process of doing so, we have almost lost touch with who God has intended for us to be. We had better wake up!

What a fearful and strange time in which we live. I get the sense of what it must have felt like for the young prophet Elisha on the day that his predecessor was carried away into the heavens.[1] He had walked for such a time with the elder that he had developed somewhat of a security underneath him. In the moment when they were "parted" the young man cried, "My father, my father!"

God was revealing to us through this instance that there would come a moment in human history when the great works of one generation and time would have to pass away, and the younger would be left to carry on. Note: The elder left the mantle which represents the anointing of God... This is enduring!

It is evident that what the elder prophet possessed was not proportioned to greet the day in which the younger would dwell, therefore God prompted and granted the young man's request for a "double portion." Then the young man cried out into the heavens, "Where is the God of Elijah?" Living in the shadows of this man will not do; "Where is the God of such men?" We need Him in our time and our day!!!

We are the ones that have so affectionately been called in recent years "Generation X." But we can no longer afford to live without definition or purpose.

Shall we define our times by standing with assurance and purpose, or shall we allow the times to define us by standing still?

We now stand at the apex of the greatest work of God ever witnessed by mortal men... And where are we?

God has apportioned to us an insight and direction unlike any other time. It would appear to the onlooker and the latecomer that we are either super-intelligent, or that God somehow skipped the generations before us and moved to something of more interest to Him. This is certainly not the case at all; but rather, it has more to do with the fact that we have actually entered into the culmination of time, for which God did reserve a special anointing and an unparalleled understanding.

The prophet Daniel saw our generation and said, **"Those who are wise [that's us] will shine like the brightness of the heavens, and those who lead many to righteousness, like the stars forever and ever" (Daniel 12:3).** Remember, however, Daniel 12:4 is very specific: "Close up the words, until the time of the end." Remember, it's not that we are more intelligent or more committed than those who have gone before us, but we are more like the generation spoken of by Jesus in the parable of the laborers. The young men lingered in the marketplace all day, waiting to be called to labor.

Herein, the words of Jesus ring true as we greet this time: "I have sent you to reap where you have not sown." No, we haven't got what others have had before us in many aspects, but we are the generations "upon whom the ends of the world have come," and if we do not step up to the plate, we will fail as representatives in a time that is most crucial to the unveiling of God's Master plan. We cannot afford leftovers, or secondhand experiences in a time that demands that we must know for ourselves who Jesus is and who we are in HIM. Time is of the essence; this world needs firsthand experience, and we can no longer afford to place men and women in positions of leadership and vision who are living off of an experience that does not even belong to them. Entrusting such a people to lead us into a land and time that they are totally out of touch with would be disastrous.

THE CHANGING OF THE GUARDS

It has been very difficult for all of us to make the necessary transitions of our time. It not only requires carefulness of thought, but swiftness of action. In the changing of the guards, we must be ever so careful and aware of our surroundings, nothing can be lost through the process.

Standing at the Tomb of the Unknown Soldier in Arlington Cemetery to witness the changing of the guards, it was absolutely amazing to learn about the rigorous hours of training and preparation that go into a transaction that takes a matter of minutes. But they MUST get it right on behalf of those who were called on before them; it is not a time to be careless. We must take the same caution and care in the changing of guards concerning this precious truth. One solider must be cognizant of the other, and both must be cognizant of the sacrifices made by those who have gone before us.

This is an hour of urgency that requires that we enter certain arenas and realms of public view and interest that we were once unfamiliar and uncomfortable with. We must take caution in each step and stride. We cannot confuse ourselves into thinking that just because the methods must change, that the message must also. Two generations must connect for one ceremony in this ultimate changing of the guards. The prophet Malachi spoke of a time just prior to a manifestation of God. This is a parallel and a picture of what God is doing in our time.

"Behold, I will send you Elijah the prophet before the great and terrible day of the LORD comes. And he will turn the hearts of fathers to their children and the hearts of children to their fathers, lest I come and smite the land with a curse." (Malachi 4:5, 6) – RSV

The sending of Elijah spoken of here is not only a prophecy of the time when John the Baptist came preaching, preparing the way for the Lord, but it is also a symbol of the spirit of revival and awakening that prepares the way of God into the hearts of men. This spirit of awakening will "turn the heart of the fathers to the children as well as the children to their fathers... lest the earth be smitten with a curse." This Scripture gives us a much clearer picture of this changing of the guard and the transaction that is taking place in our time. The spiritual fathers must be aware of those upon whom the mantle of God is falling, and they with their hearts must turn and trust that God has equipped these children, imputing upon them their wisdom and strength.

Again, the turning of the hearts of the children to the fathers is a picture of the respect and honor due those who have given birth to us and have gone before to pave the way. We must carry on the precious and necessary, and respectfully exchange what has been useful in times past for that which will be useful in our times.

One precious elder was speaking some time ago concerning this great transition, saying, "I'm glad we are not where we were, but there are a few things I wished we would be more careful to bring with us along the way."[1] There is a great danger in transition; the message cannot change, but the world in which we live will. Therefore, our methods must change with the times. We must hold near the things that are enduring and fit them to our time... Truth is truth, no matter what language or generation you speak it in.

In times of such transition, we are in need of leadership that will fearlessly step up to meet the challenges of our times without compromising the foundations of our experience, yet flexible enough to exchange their personal opinions of operation for an up-to-date version of the truth that the world can relate to, live by, and understand.

There will be perils and difficulties, no doubt; confusions, frustrations, and misunderstandings. We've all heard concerns and complaints from both the passing and the coming generations, but we cannot afford to falter.

One can almost hear the crowd as Joshua took the place of the great leader Moses: "Who does that kid think he is?" "Does he think he's smarter or better than Moses?" The answer was NO, but he is called and equipped of God to carry you into the land of promise, so don't knock it. The passing generation had to trust what God had placed within him, as well trust the position that God had placed him in, or it would find great difficulty in crossing over into the land of promise. The same is true in our generation.

FOR WHOM THE BELL TOLLS

"The glory of the latter shall be greater than the former..." These are the words of promise and they fall to the end time generation, [the "latter house," if you please]. The time is upon us, this is not up for bids, trades, or handoffs; it belongs to us and we must prepare to embrace it with all of our might! We are that latter house. Others may have carelessly drifted through their times, but now it's "HIGH TIME," and we cannot take it for granted.

Our time calls for proven, God-ordained ministry that will not settle for some temporary fix or position just to appease their ego or agenda. We need men and women who have already counted the cost and are ready to pay the price; souls are dying! In the first part of this chapter, we reflected on the transition between the prophets Elijah and Elisha. And you will notice that when the younger asked for the double portion, the elder's comment was simply, "You have asked a hard thing." Notice that though it was hard, the youngster did not retract his request. He asked on, he followed on; choosing rather to be fit for the work of God than to be subtracted from the turmoil that often surrounds such labor and commitment. This is the kind of resolve and determination that we are going to need to lead our generation.

For those who have danced around the edges of greatness for so long, here is wisdom: *"The difficult is not the impossible."* The excuses are over! Just because things of God may be difficult to access, it does not make them impossible. The Lord has designed the deeper things to be a bit difficult to press into, to protect the access of such things from the casual and careless. Consistency and commitment are not only the avenues to the ways of the works of the Spirit, but they are also the best guardians. Such characteristics stand constant watch of the priceless works of God, guarding them from those who would only propagate His works for their own wealth, fame, and glory.

As the younger prophet was not satisfied to dwell in his smallness and the shadow of his predecessor, we should not be satisfied to dwell in a portion that belongs to days gone by. It is time to move on. Just as the young prophet was faithful and followed the course of the elder keeping the pace, we too must obtain that same faithful passion and keep the pace. As the moment of transition came and they were "parted," one was left to the ages, and the other to the age at hand. The younger, being the future, was not silent or still for very long, but rather he took what he had learned from the former and began to put it into motion for himself in his generation.

As the younger took the mantle and turned to the same river that his predecessor had crossed just a while before him, he cried out, "Where is the God of Elijah?" We too must turn with holy zeal and covet earnestly the same gifts and calling. No more can we dwell in the covert of another man's labor alone; we must arise and call for ourselves, "Where is the God of our fathers?"

CHAPTER FOUR

UNFOUNDED FEARS

"Don't talk to strangers!" we were always advised as kids. And thus, as we grew, everyone and everything that we were not familiar with, we feared. Anything that we did not know for ourselves became our enemy, and through the process of time, the enemy has drawn us right into his trap. In the age of terror, fear and torment without confrontation are freedom's greatest enemies. *Fear of the battle and its great unknown has crippled more men than the weapons of warfare ever will.*

We must remember that the great unknown things of our time, which could easily cause our hearts to tremble, belong to God. Too many have missed "today," for fear of looking after tomorrow. The thing about tomorrow is that it is not ours anyway! Today is the only day that we have any power over!

"And there shall be signs in the sun, and in the moon, and in the stars; and upon the earth distress of nations, with perplexity; the sea and the waves roaring; <u>men's hearts failing them for fear, and for looking after those things which are coming on the earth:</u> for the powers of heaven shall be shaken." (Luke 21:25, 26)

Our times belong to God; we cannot allow the enemy of our soul through fear to intimidate and disqualify us. It's time to move onto the scene. We are prisoners of a time and a world we have no control over, when we fear tomorrow. We cannot fear to go out and go on from this point forward. We must stand up in faith, and step out into the unknown with boldness, trusting that the Hand of God is upon us to accomplish His purpose. Listen to the Lord's advice for our times:

"You will hear of wars and rumors of wars: SEE THAT YOU ARE NOT TROUBLED: for all these things must come to pass, but the end is not yet. Nations will rise against nations, Kingdoms against kingdoms: and there will be famines and sicknesses, and earthquakes in some of the most unexpected places on earth." (Matthew 24:6, 7)

These things "must come to pass." This is God's way of helping us to understand that such things belong to the age just as we do. There are things that must come to pass because they are a part of the unfolding of God's will, and we cannot allow them to distract us! We've lived a sheltered life for quite some time in this generation, and it's all because our forefathers fought to make sure that we wouldn't have to suffer as they did to obtain. Their motives were pure and innocent; the outcome however, has proven to leave us quite vulnerable in a time greater than our forefathers have ever faced. Preparing his generation for war, President Franklin D. Roosevelt said it well in his address to the nation on the eve of conflict, "There is nothing to fear but fear itself." He couldn't have been more right. Once the enemy sees that we fear to face the great unknown before us, without ever laying a finger, he has won!

A friend of mine was an officer in the KGB during the cold war. He told me how they would torture and even kill people without laying a hand on them. He told me that every day the prisoners would be taken out randomly. Blindfolded, the prisoners would be told to walk the secret passageway underground while the agent would walk a few paces behind. Each time they were taken out, they would walk the mile journey while the guard would hold an empty gun near the prisoner's head and every now and then, pull the trigger. (The gun, being empty, would not go off.)

For days, they would repeat this routine, breaking down the resistance of the prisoner, building upon the fear of the unknown. On the last day of the process, the guards would take the prisoners on the same journey as days before, only this time with no weapon at all. In silence, they would walk, and as they would reach the end of their journey, the guard would simply clap his hands together as loudly as possible. At that moment, the prisoner, at the mercy of fear and the unknown, having been worn down in resistance, would drop over dead of heart failure.

The enemy has tried this with our generation; the prophet Daniel said that he would seek to "wear out the saints," but we must not allow him! The things that are coming upon us belong to the times in which we live; not to us, and NOT to the enemy of our soul! Remember, "These things must come to pass." They are part of a cycle and they will not stay. Why should we let our hearts be overwhelmed trying to keep up with times that are only temporary?

The Apostle Paul's advice to the church of the time in which we dwell was very fitting, "...be not soon shaken in mind, or be troubled, neither by spirit, nor by word, nor by letter..." (2 Thessalonians 2:2). There will be wars, and rumors of wars. There will be fearful sights around us, but we cannot live in constant fear. These things belong to the age in which we live. In such times, let us constantly be reminded of the words of Jesus:

"In this world you will have trouble, but be of good cheer, I have overcome the world" (John 16:33).

CHAPTER FIVE

A SUBPOENA FOR THE SAVIOR

The lonely God of the universe accepted His summons to the courtroom of mankind and his constant misunderstanding. (It wasn't the first time.) A sudden barrage of interrogation was hurled relentlessly against the Creator of the world, like the prosecution and cross-examination of a downtown murder trial lawyer. The questions came without respect and without ceasing. The worst of it all was that many were called to appear as His character witnesses, and yet the courtroom of humanity was barren, meanwhile God had been called to the stand...

"Where were YOU on the morning of September 11?" "Where were YOU the day the federal building in Oklahoma City was bombed?" And "Where were YOU, God, the day Columbine High School became a war zone and thirteen innocent young souls died?" "Where were YOU on Christmas Day 2004 when the Tsunami raged across the Indian Ocean killing thousands of unsuspecting people?" On and on the questions are fired in an endless torrent of accusation and blame. You can read the accusative language in the paper, and you can hear it in the tone of every reporter's voice; there are a lot of questions and a lot of unfounded fears.

To question is human, this is true; it may not always be valid, but it is normal. But I think it necessary at this point to remind the reader that "[WE] are the body of Christ..." (1 Corinthians 12:27). In modern vernacular, simply stated, "We are the only 'GOD' the world will ever see." Therefore, this assiduous assault concerning the character and whereabouts of God in moments of world crisis and catastrophe is actually an indictment against the church of our time. If you and I are going to operate as true Christians and fulfill the Great Commission, this indictment must be taken personally. In a predominantly deistic society, it is an absolute disgrace to the Kingdom of Heaven on earth to have the God of our forefathers called to witness stand while we (the body of Christ) stand innocently by. The world needs to know that God is constantly involved and concerned with the affairs of mankind. As Grover Cleveland so eloquently put it, **"I know there is a Supreme Being who rules the affairs of men and whose goodness and mercy have always followed the American people, and I know He will not turn from us now if we humbly and reverently seek His powerful aid."[1]**

Earthly residents had no problem finding God in the days of the first church, as He would oft manifest Himself through the disciples. But when this generation starts crying out, "Where's God when we need Him?" I think it's time to take an inventory of who we are and what we are professing. It would be safe to say at this point that what's really happening here is a wake-up call in the house of God. When God is called to the carpet, what is really happening here is that WE "the BODY," were not where we could have been or should have been in their time of need. **CODE ADAM!**

THE TRUE CHARACTER WITNESS

We are the ambassadors (or representatives) of a Kingdom far beyond the boundaries of this world and time. All of this Kingdom's power and authority is expressed through us, the CHURCH. The responsibility was laid upon us the moment that Jesus Christ handed the keys to the Apostle Peter and said, **"I will give unto thee the keys of the kingdom of heaven: and whatsoever thou shalt bind on earth shall be bound in heaven: and whatsoever thou shalt loose on earth shall be loosed in heaven"** (Matthew 16:19). Thus, Heaven was accessed by and through this man, and ultimately the CHURCH.

We are the "image of the invisible God"[2] to this present world. So when we hear the world turn to Him in anger, rage, despair, and utter hopelessness, it should grip us once and for all. This is not about God and His whereabouts, because frankly, He never moves out of His place! It is time that an alert signal is sent out into our generation... As we near the end of the age, there are certain to be many more tragedies. Although there may not be anything that we can do to stop them, we must recognize our place in the aftermath.

CASE IN POINT:

The story of the poor man who sat at the pool called Bethesda, having an infirmity for thirty-eight years has always intrigued me. It's interesting to note that there were many "religious folk" who passed him by to get to the waters for themselves and to go about all their other business, or maybe there were even wealthier folks who paid others to see to it that their loved one was the first to enter the water when it was troubled. Whatever the case, notice that if it hadn't been for the fact that God was walking the earth that day in the MAN CHRIST JESUS, the poor man would have died there by the pool of possibility.

Listen to what the lame man said: "I have no **man**, when the water is troubled, to put me into the pool..." (John 5:7). There is no deficit of God here in this picture, but this man needed more than a good word or thought, he needed a literal hand. The Apostle Peter said to the man sitting at the "Beautiful Gate," "Look at us." Why? Because when you see me, you ought to be able to see JESUS the healer, the provider, and the miracle worker! *I wonder what the world sees when those who are in need look to our direction?* God's ability to operate in the earth is expressed through His body, the church! The Bible said the man at the temple gate "gave heed, expecting to receive something." The man had been looking for something a little more than what he had previously known, and this day he found it! Paul said that it is "Christ IN YOU, the hope of glory."

Before someone gets completely offended, let me say in defense of those of us who have dedicated our lives to reflecting the person and the power of Jesus, that there are those who would not even accept Him if He did work a miracle in their midst. It is impossible for God to work beyond the bounds of willful rejection; He's too much of a gentleman. There are those who have resisted His love and existence in their "good days" and quite frankly, they should not expect His assistance in the evil day (God rarely commits to the uncommitted). I think if ever God was hard for people to locate, it was because He was probably hiding Himself long enough to dry the tears from His eyes after having been rejected.

It is truly sad, but there are those who have put Him so far into the background of their lives that in a time of true need, they turn to call, only to find out how far behind they have left Him. For these, we can only hope and pray... But for those who call on Him in hunger and despair, we are called to be their light.

A CLOSER LOOK

So where is God and how do so many even among the ranks of Christendom miss Him? They miss Him because they do not rightfully "discern the body." There are times and moments when He has made Himself available, and still He was not received because of the condition that He was revealed in. Here's an example: He was born in a manger, to a young mother who came from a relatively poor family. John says, "He came unto HIS OWN, and they received Him not." Why, because of how He was revealed.

The world of that time thought that the Messiah would reveal Himself as a true king in pomp and splendor, riding in a golden chariot, driven by the finest horses. Instead, Jesus came walking everywhere He went, and the only time he rode anything was when he rode into Jerusalem on a donkey to ultimately be crucified! His "elite" were sinner folk, and fishermen. His greatest messages of fury were directed and preached to the religious, while most of the other time, He was found having dinner with sinners and publicans.

The angel who accompanied the ascension of Christ told the disciples standing by: "This SAME JESUS whom you have seen taken up into the clouds will return in like manner." I like that wording, this "SAME JESUS." The world would think to place some other identity upon Him in our time, and the enemy would love to confuse those who are sincerely looking for Him. We are assured, however, that He will be in no other condition when He

David Bryan

returns for His church than when He ascended on that day into the heavens.

I speak this to our awakening church because if He is not recognizable to us and through us, then there is no way He will be recognizable to the world around us! We must profess and express that "SAME JESUS."

Peter and John walked with Him on the day of His resurrection, but they did not know who He was, His own disciples! Oh, death and persecution have a way of quickly causing men to lose sight and hope of the true reality and identity of Jesus. The Bible says that they thought He was a stranger. In another place, Mary thought He was just one of the gardeners. How possibly could they have missed Him? After all, hadn't they spent three years with Him face to face? Here's the key: "Their eyes were holden" (or kept from recognizing Him) (Luke 24:16).

A more literal interpretation of the Scripture helps us to understand that their vision was clouded and distorted. There was a literal haze within their mental and physical atmosphere. They didn't recognize Him because He took on a form that was quite different than what they had become accustomed to.

I think we are on to something here... It is sad to say that in our ranks, Jesus has taken on a form contrary to what we are comfortable or accustomed to in our self-made religious community of ideas, and we too have missed some mighty manifestations. We like to believe that we have a handle on what He would and would not look like, or how He would talk, or where He might go, or what He might say or do. But because His thoughts are "higher than our thoughts, and His ways are higher than our ways," we do not always know. So where's God? Well, He may not be that far away. Phillip said, "Okay Jesus, show me the Father and we'll call it good and settle this conflict in my mind once and for all." Jesus, answering him said, "Phillip, have I stood this long in your midst and you still don't know who I am?" (John 14:8,9 additions mine).

In our times, we have done much the same in the church world. We pray, "God we want revival, we want You to move in our midst; do whatever You must and through whomever You will..." So He does it and then we say, "There's no way that could have been God.

34

I don't even know who that preacher is, and besides that, none of his family is in church." On and on we go dismissing some of the greatest works of God in our time. Well, I for one am not going to miss it! What more can God do if He's been there working all along and they still haven't gotten it?

Not believing in His ability to manifest Himself on multiple levels as an omnipotent, omniscient, and omnipresent God does not keep Him from being God; it only keeps those who refuse to see Him working from being able to appreciate what He can and will do in their midst.

We have such preconceived ideas of who God is and how He would and should reveal Himself to us in our service to Him. Jesus spoke to a generation similar to the one we dwell in and said, **"I was hungry and you didn't feed me, I was thirsty and you gave me nothing to drink, and I appeared as a stranger dressed differently and speaking differently than your kind and you wouldn't take Me in. I had no clothes to wear and you assumed it was because of choices that I had made, and I was sick and in prison, but you wanted nothing to do with my kind" (Matthew 25:41-45 KJV, additions mine).** He's getting closer all the time, isn't He?

So where is God now, you say...? **"Inasmuch as you have done it unto the least of these my brethren, you have done it unto ME" (Matthew 25:40).** The religious and inquisitive of Jesus's day were asking "where, why, when, who, and how." His answer was quite interesting: "The Kingdom of God comes not with observation" or as the Living Bible states, "...it is not ushered in with visible signs" (Luke 17:20, 21). God's Kingdom does not always operate in visible and easily understandable ways. You will not always be able to say, "It's over here or over there." The true understanding of the operation of God and His Kingdom is from within you. When we hear the Psalmist saying, "Let God arise," we can now further understand that he is talking to a people who by relationship hold the power to know Him and reveal Him from within. Think about that! We have the power to access (or locate) Him and release Him into the world, and we must do so from within the walls of personal relationship and understanding. By simply understanding this and helping others to understand, a door of great revelation can be opened unto our generation.

To locate God is to locate one's own experience (the Kingdom of Heaven is truly within), so instead of asking "Where are You, God?" ask yourself, "Where did I put Him?" Chances are He's right where you left Him.

The real question then here, Adam, is... "Where were you?"

CHAPTER SIX

CODE ADAM (WHERE ART THOU?)

The doors to the store suddenly lock. The frantic call comes forth over the loudspeakers: "**CODE ADAM** to all personnel." Suddenly, every store employee from the stockmen to the sales clerk immediately deploy as a search party. A child is missing on the premises; he must be found before it's too late! In the introduction of this book, I briefly mentioned the Adam Walsh story. This story and countless others are heard nearly daily in our time. Child abductions, innocent lives robbed of future hope. As the author of this project it is my distinct pleasure and what's more, my mandate to see to it that the same cry that sent common men and women to search for children they've never really known, would go out into the church world and into this generation as a spiritual emergency code that would employ the hearts of the casual to action! Some of the future greats of God's church are missing and we must locate them! **CODE ADAM**

If it is true (and it is) that we are the body of Christ, and that we are the ones who are currently responsible for the manifestation of the power and glory of God in this generation, then we've got an emergency on our hands, because the halls and aisles of Kingdom operation are nearly empty... Adam, "Where art thou?" It's time for a total lockdown in Christianity of today; we must employ whomever available and whatever means necessary to find those among us who will help to redefine this priceless generation and bring in as many lost souls as possible! The world needs us now more than ever. We have been asleep for too long. It is time that we take responsibility for our location. Where are you?

Maybe the real question we should ask ourselves is "Where were we?" Nobody will forget where they were on September 11, 2001, but how many of us remember where we were or what was on our minds on September 9, (which, incidentally, was a Sunday, the perfect setup for the continuation of our subject matter, "judgment must begin at the House of God.")

Go back and think about it — where were you? What was on your mind? What was your level of commitment to God at that time? Who were you angry with? What was the message about? Did you pray any differently? Were you promoting a program or going through motions? Where were you on that day?

Missing from the place of God's complete purpose in my life, there I sat in the house of God September 9, 2001. I had no idea that our whole world would drastically change within the next forty-eight hours. God was speaking that day, but I, along with many others, wasn't really tuned in. Little did we know, the times that God had prepared the church for were about to converge upon us with great intensity, and His most valuable resource was missing. The body of Christ had lost touch with reality along the way, and now here we sat on the eve of end time fulfillment, about to miss out on the very reason we were born into this generation. "Adam, where art thou?"

SOME THINGS NEVER CHANGE

Jesus lived in a time when men were asking some of the same questions we ask today. Jesus came one day into the temple, turning tables and casting out money changers, because the religious of the time simply had lost focus with who they were as a people and what they were supposed to be doing. Some things just never change. Here we are, thousands of years later, and if Jesus were to walk into many of our lives or church services today, I fear there would be some scourging and that He would find much the same as He did in His day.

Maybe the question should be asked to the church world of today, "Where art thou?" This is a question posed to the generation that boasts of legal abortion and still sentences men to prison for murder; a generation laden with immoral extremity; parents molesting children, same-sex marriage, and lawless youth running wild in the streets, meanwhile their parents drink themselves into oblivion somewhere, "Where art thou?" When wrong is right, and church board meetings become slander sessions, and song service tryouts for 'American Idol,' "Adam where art thou?"

We've run long enough from reality. Our times are out of whack and it's high time that somebody brought things into proper perspective. **CODE ADAM.**

If we are nowhere to be found in this, the world's greatest hour of need, then God has an emergency on His Hands. Where are you, Adam? The human race, the crown of God's creative plan, the one through whom He had designed and determined to cultivate and fulfill His ultimate will; what have you had to do that was more important than answering the voice of your Father?

"Where are you, Adam? I have heard your cry," says the Lord. "You said you wanted revival, you have cried out for fresh oil and new wine; you said you would go anywhere, do anything, and speak to anyone without fear or favor. You've cried for unity, and yet I find you in no fellowship with others. I have heard your plea for the lost of your own household, but I cannot find you among them. You've prayed for direction and refuse to follow, sought for peace and refuse to comfort others. Where art thou?"

A VOICE FROM DAYS GONE BY

The first "**CODE ADAM**" ever issued was in the Garden of Eden in the beginning of time. A relationship once untouched by sin and selfish motive was destroyed in a moment's time. Adam never had to ask where God was, and God never had to seek the whereabouts of Adam; the two were inseparable. When sin entered the picture, the scene dramatically changed. God was not the one hard to find, however, Adam was. Sin had kidnapped him, robbed him of his God-given identity. What a tragedy, because the very earth that he was entrusted to dress and to keep will now be left to the elements of sin. Can you hear the Father's cry, "Adam, where are you?"

Adam represents the New Testament generation of the God called and re-created; appointed, anointed, and reserved to "Keep and dress" the "Garden of God." There are certain moments of history (this being one of them) when God steps in just to check up on His investments, as He did in the beginning of time in the Garden. What He expects to find is that which He had instituted from the beginning in the midst of operation. An alteration in the original instruction warrants the judgment of God. Thus, it is written, **"Blessed is that servant whom the Lord finds doing when he comes," or as The Living Bible states, "Blessings on you if I (the Lord) return and find you faithfully doing the work He created and called you to do" (Matthew 24:46 additions mine).**

The prophet Ezekiel recorded another time when God looked in on humanity for a chosen vessel and "found none." How could one who was kept so near to the heart of God, and was created to be so powerful, just come up missing? Well, look at Adam's answer from the beginning: **"I heard Your voice walking in the garden so I hid myself" (Genesis 3:10).** Notice, he was close enough to know that God was nearby, and even discerned His voice, yet he hid himself because in his heart, sin had taken him far from his original state of being, and he was ashamed of who he had become; sin had condemned him and withdrawn him from potential in the presence of God.

Sin and condemnation had tricked Adam into believing that he was totally useless and unacceptable to God; therefore, the only thing he could do to cover his shame was run and hide...

"...BECAUSE I WAS AFRAID..."

Afraid, you say, Adam... Afraid of what, Failures of your past, rejection of those who love you, the unknown, or maybe the truth? Believe it or not, there is a whole generation that is completely missing from the map of usefulness in God's most desperate hour because they are "afraid." A whole generation of potential teachers, preachers, missionaries, evangelists, and SOUL WINNERS Gone off the map, missing from action, hidden because they are afraid.

Adam's answer rings true today. "I was afraid because I was naked." Now, God made you this way, Adam; since when did this become wrong? What wrong have you done with the things that God has created in innocence? My question to today's Adam is this: "Who told you that who you are now is useless? Who told you that you have failed God one time too many?" It was obvious when God asked the question that Adam had been listening to someone else. He was listening to a lie!

The prophet Isaiah says, "We have made lies our refuge (or covering), under falsehood have we hid ourselves" (Isaiah 28:15). In another place, the prophet says, "...we hid (as it were) our faces from Him; He was despised and we esteemed Him not." (Isaiah 53:3) These are desperate times in God's economy. Who else is going to keep this great Garden of God, and what right do we have disqualifying ourselves or anyone else from service? We have no more right to disqualify ourselves for service to God than other men do... NONE at all! God is the only one who qualifies and disqualifies... You have no excuse! Adam, where are you?

Think about it. A whole generation is silent from operation because they have somehow been supposedly disqualified for service? Whether they condemned themselves or allowed others to condemn them, it is not known, but one thing is for certain: If they have condemned themselves, "God is greater than their own heart and condemnation" (1 John 3:20). And if other men condemn us, be it known that no man has the power to vote the call of God in or out of anyone's life. No man has the power to disqualify that which has been approved of old. "No man has the power to pluck them out of My Father's hand" (John 10:29).

God is in the process right now of instituting and restoring to usefulness some of the greatest ministry of all time. That's what this call is all about. **CODE ADAM** is all about the missing, and all about God's urgent attempt to locate them and activate them as quickly as possible! Come out from beneath your personal fears and ideologies. Come out from the prison of tradition and religiosity. It is time that we recognize the gifts and the calling among us and upon us. It's time to strengthen one another to operate. God said, "What I have cleansed *for service* is not to be called [or placed among the] common." You may recognize those words, these were the words spoken to the Apostle Peter to prepare him for the fact that God was getting ready to allow that which He knew others would not be comfortable with or understand. Soon the whole world could experience what was once confined to a single group of people. And so the call goes out today, "Adam, where are you?" God is preparing an ultimate generation; are you ready?

CHAPTER SEVEN

SLEEPING GIANTS

Did you ever notice that the alarm clock always rings when sleep feels best? Then, of course, there's always that party wrecker who bursts through the door to reaffirm the reality to what we'd hoped was only a dream... "It's time to get up!"

As a teenager, these were some of the most dreaded words of my day; life is just so much better when no one bothers us while we are sleeping, isn't it?

As a teen, my time was precious to me; there were friends to see, places to go, and things to do, but on my time. I had my own schedule to keep and my own timeframe in which to keep it. I didn't want anyone rushing me into my day, especially when sleep felt sooooo good. Looking back on some of the sleep-ins of my past, it's a bit disheartening to think that I could have slept through some of the most important days of my life, but hey, my clock was always right [so I thought].

If you are one of those casual, sleepy Christians, you're probably not going to want to hear this, but this is the voice of God to the church of our generation... "GET UP and get involved!" Maybe you will recall the account when Jacob, the great patriarch of Israel, camped in a place one night and took stones for a pillow. The Scripture reveals that when he awoke from "his sleep," he realized that God had been there. He realized a little too late, however, and I believe this is why he was so insistent at the wrestling match that he had a little later on in his life; I am sure he had determined not to miss it again. God is merciful; He gave him another chance.

Notice in the story of Jacob's ladder that the Scripture is careful to reveal that it was "his sleep" and not God's rest that kept him from being truly aware that where he was camping that night was the gate of Heaven! What an awful thing to wake up and find out you were sleeping right at the doorway of possibility, but too tired to enter! There is a difference between divine rest and human slumber. Divine rest is productive; human slumber (which symbolizes carnality, carelessness, and laxity) is actually degenerative, and destructive to the work of the Spirit of God in our life.

"For they that are after the flesh do mind the things of the flesh; but they that are after the Spirit the things of the Spirit. For to be carnally minded is death; but to be spiritually minded is life and peace. Because the carnal mind is enmity against God: for it is not subject to the law of God, neither indeed can be" (Romans 8:5-7 KJV).

Here is productive sleep; after God created man, He caused a "deep sleep" to fall upon Adam, and created for him a help mate. This is divine rest, and it was productive. In Genesis 15, the Lord caused the same kind of sleep to fall upon the patriarch Abram and it was productive as well: "...the LORD made a covenant with Abram, saying, unto thy seed have I given this land."

We find quite the opposite in the New Testament, when men fall prey to their own carnal slumber. The apostle speaks to our generation saying, "It's HIGH TIME that we awake from sleep." We've been asleep for far too long; it's time to move, it's time to take action. It's time that we are seen and heard on the courthouse steps, and on the Capitol lawn. *A message that has no bounds should be preached by a people who are not afraid to cross them!* If we were to crawl back into our little religious bed of slumber at this point, we would only be aiding and empowering the wicked of our time. Or as one has said, **"The only thing necessary for the triumph of evil is for good men to do nothing."**[1] Silence, slumber, and lack of interest or involvement have done more damage to the gospel in recent years than a sea of tyrants, and all hell with both hands could ever dream of doing. It's time to wake up!

We do not need the signs in the heavens and the earth to know what time it is. We do not need prophecy up-dates, the Apostle Paul wrote to the church and said, "you know perfectly that the day of the Lord will come as a thief in the night" (1 Thessalonians 5:2). We have been mistaken in recent years by watching the signs of our times, and then charting our course. But signs are for those who yet need convincing; we who are already convinced should already be in place so that when these things do take place we can move into action.

We've complained because "they" have taken prayer out of school, and "they" have legalized the murder of millions of unborn children. "They" are flaunting their immoral lives before us, and "they" are slowly over taking our judicial system; while we do what?? Sleep? I don't think so! hell would love for some of us to sleep a few more hours! Notice in the parable of the tares sown among the wheat, the farmer asks, "how did this happen?" The answer came forth clearly: "While men slept!"

The truth of the matter is that the only reason that *"THEY"* have any power at all is because WE have been asleep for too long!

"Another parable put He forth unto them, saying, The kingdom of heaven is likened unto a man which sowed good seed in his field: But while men slept, his enemy came and sowed tares among the wheat, and went his way. But when the blade was sprung up, and brought forth fruit, then appeared the tares also. So the servants of the householder came and said unto him, Sir, didst not thou sow good seed in thy field? From whence then hath it tares? He said unto them, an enemy hath done this" (Matthew 13:24-28).

It's time to get up! The only reason that many of the powers that have overtaken our time have been at all successful is because we have slept in too long! It's time to get up! We argue about our differences with the church across town. We fight and fuss about each other and what true Christianity is all about. Meanwhile, there is a whole world going on around us into which we have been commissioned to go and preach the gospel. It's time to wake up!

WAKE UP THE MIGHTY MEN

There is a great army sleeping among us, an army so great that when they awaken, it will catch the known world, the church world, and the powers of hell by great surprise. Joel spoke to the Gentiles, saying to them, "Wake up the mighty men." "Now wait a minute," says the typical churchgoer, "I thought God would only use us four and no more; the holy, the perfect, and pure." "What do you mean God is speaking to the Gentiles, aren't they the refuse and the unacceptable?!"

Well, God did say he would call a people who were "not a people" and make them a great people of God, didn't He? Well, here are the facts: there are among us, God called and chosen people in this generation who have either never known or have once known the power of God and have been rocked to sleep by the powers of darkness. The Word of the Lord is coming to them in our time, awakening them to Divine purpose. Maybe you are one of them, and you have grown callous and cold, weary and worn waiting on God's promise to be fulfilled in your life. So you've just given up and have fallen back from the original plan. Well, friend, God has been looking everywhere for you, He needs you now! Maybe you know somebody personally that God has been preparing through tribulation and rejection. If so, maybe God will speak through you into their life... We must awaken them to the times and the plans of God. "Provoke them to good works." Encourage them unto fulfillment of God's purpose in their life...

Eagles are majestic birds of war, and freedom. They represent power, wisdom, and security. Interestingly enough, however, when two or more of them get together for any amount of time, they will actually start tearing one another apart! What a disappointing sight that would be, to see such respected creatures dissolving to such base nature and activity. Man, on the other hand, was not made to be alone, but rather dependant one upon another, Adam's Dad said, **"It is not good to be alone."** The sad thing is, however, that even in the church world, we haven't been able to work together for too long before we are actually doing the same thing as these majestic birds! I fear that many of the missing of our time we may find like the lost coin in the parable spoken by the Lord "...lost in the house." We must learn to work together; God's Kingdom is plural, not singular, and the *body* as Paul says, "has many members." It has been said that "No man is an island, entire of itself; every man is a piece of the continent, a part of the main;"[2] or as the great motivational speaker Dennis Waitley stated,

"To exist just for yourself is meaningless. You can achieve the most satisfaction when you feel related to some greater purpose in life, something greater than yourself."[3]

We need one another; this is how we survive as a "body." It is truly time to wake up the mighty among us. We have allowed some very foolish things to cause us to lose focus in recent times, and we have in many cases killed and eaten even our own. Wake up! If we would fight hell the way some of us fight one another, we would have victory and understanding in many more spiritual dimensions than we do now!

Speaking of conflict within Christendom, doctrine seems to have been a popular battleground as of late. But to the true professing Christian, basic Bible doctrine should be one of the last areas of struggle. There is only one doctrine, the doctrine of Christ. There is "ONE LORD, ONE FAITH, and ONE BAPTISM," so what's the argument over? Anything that confirms and reaffirms such is called TRUTH; anything that opposes this is error, so what's the fuss over? Before you jump into your next theological debate, remember this as well; The Word of God is secure within itself. Man is only called to defend what he has created for himself. It would be sad to know how many have foolishly spiritually died or killed others trying to prove their own point.

God's church is bigger than a building, bigger than a city, and certainly bigger than our ego. Oh God, wake us up! It's no wonder the force and fierceness of Jesus's preaching was largely directed toward the religious of His day. These supposed holy men spent so much time caught up in their own little world that they missed a once-in-a-lifetime visitation.

"He was in this world and He made the world, and yet they did not know Him" (John 1:10). And why didn't they know Him? Because they were asleep. They were asleep when God came to dwell among them, and asleep when He prayed in the garden in the most crucial moment of salvation's history. God help us that we not slumber any longer and miss the greatest opportunity of all. Somebody wake up the mighty men!

CHAPTER EIGHT

BEFORE THE ROCKS CRY OUT!

The streets were filled with hopeful onlookers and supporters the day of the Lord's triumphal entry into Jerusalem.[1] Jubilation and hope filled the air as the King of Glory descended upon the City of Truth. Suddenly, in an unfortunate display of prejudice and envy, the supposed religious of His day began to cry out against this public display of emotion and affection. "Shut these people up, they are destroying our agenda, they are wrecking our plans!" No sooner did their venomous attempt to silence the heart cry of the sincere come forth, when Jesus turned in divine rebuke toward them, exclaiming, "If these should hold their peace, the rocks would cry out in their place." "If these," who are "these," and what makes their cry so special and so different that God Himself would defend them? These are they who as Daniels says, "Understand among the people." These are they who know and believe, and if they should fall silent, all creation and history will rise up and speak in their place!

Speaking of not holding our peace, we are hearing some of the greatest preaching ever heard and in places where the voice of God was once silenced. A fresh, fearless voice is coming forth with great boldness! We are seeing the Word of God that was once confined to the sanctuary, now begin to fill the streets of our great nation; it's a new day here in North America, and in the church world, we've got something to say and we are going to be heard! Everyone else has had their chance to speak, and now it's our turn. (We'll talk more about this in the next chapter.)

It seemed for so long that every time someone among us would dare to stand up and speak anything different than what the larger population has defined as common, we would be silenced by the corrupt voice of the "majority rule." But now the voices of our gospel fathers can fear to fade no more. A generation forced to silence by our own guilt, shame, and foolishness finally has something to say, and we will be heard!

This is our finest hour to speak, so let's say it, say it loud, and say it clear! It's time the casual religious understand that it does take true commitment to God to survive in these times! It takes dedication, consecration, and purity of mind, soul, body, and spirit. It's time to tell the God scoffers that though He chastens, He does love, He can save, and HE IS COMING AGAIN! Let's tell the immoral that sex outside of the bonds of matrimony is wrong in God's eyes, homosexuality is an abomination, lying still warrants hell, and prejudice is sickening in the eyes of God.

Why should we be silent? We have more certain evidence in our day than any other generation before us that God is up to something great. Since the beginning of this new millennium, history has dramatically changed course. One of the most pivotal dates of our time is of course September 11, 2001. For those who are not aware of what God is really up to at this time, this date (as well as others hereafter) has been used as a weapon against the people and the plan of God on several occasions concerning the time in which we now reside in prophetically.

A perfect example of its misuse was an article in my local newspaper claiming that: "LESS BELIEVE IN GOD NOW THAN BEFORE 9/11." I was so troubled by this that I decided to take it upon myself to help them to understand where we really are, so I wrote my own piece. Let them have their say, that's fine; freedom of speech is for all (right or wrong) but why don't you print this too: We have watched in recent times as total churches have converted to truth. We've seen blind eyes open, and thousands of common people receive the gift of the Holy Ghost in mass crusades and rallies. How about that for headlines?! Evidence from where we stand declares that more have come to believe in God since the beginning of the new millennium, and more will come to know the Lord within the very near future, more than ever before in human history! Why do I believe this to be so? Because aside from statistics alone, there is a tangible hunger worldwide for the things of God that can be charted and proven in several ways.

First of all, you will note the "conservative" mindset of the people in this last presidential election. Secondly we are seeing a return to core values within the conservative educational community. Thirdly, we find attendance to churches, and major conferences, conventions, and crusades are increasing rapidly. Such attendance to the things of God is ignited by the very events that distinctly declare our age to be "the end times." Major catastrophes typically work for and not against the work of God.

Prayer is returning to school, and college Bible study group attendance is exploding across our continent. There is a tangible feeling in the air that this generation has come into its own, and we will not be silenced or defined by the godless and corrupt of our time. Response to more recent tragedies of our time has proven and revealed once again that there is a generation among us that is truly hungry for more than social help, but for the divine.

While secular media is relentlessly trying to slant principles of truth by employing their liberal opinions and techniques, I think it's fair to warn them that there is a people who are not going to sit idly by while they create their dictionaries and doctrines for modern society. We will not be silent about what we know anymore! We've seen too much, know too much, and want too much. These are the real facts: there is a hunger for truth now more than ever before, and those who have detoured the general public so far out of the way of truth to keep people from hearing us need to know that they are about to lose their greatest audience ever!

THE TRUTH OF THE MATTER IS...

God has got this world's attention like never before, and He has given this generation a word to speak that will be heard!!! The Bible says that the prophet Daniel had a vision concerning the time that we are living in. He dreamt of three beasts, and a fourth who was more "terrible than the rest." This fourth beast comes to represent the government and the power of the anti-Christ and his kingdom in the earth during the end time. The interesting thing in this vision was that Daniel said that he came near to ask an angel near by the "truth of all this," and the Bible reveals that the angel made him to know the "interpretation of the things" (Daniel 7:16).

Well, you know as well as I do, there is a vast difference between TRUTH and interpretation. Daniel heard him say however, that the "saints of the MOST HIGH would possess the Kingdom" (that's us)... in verse 19; and then we hear Daniel say, "Then [after the saints possessed the Kingdom] I would know the TRUTH..." (Daniel 7:19). The world is full of interpretations and ideas, but TRUTH has only one source!

This is why John encouraged his disciples and said, "You have an unction from the Holy One, and you know all things" (1 John 2:20). Jesus is that Holy One, and He is the "WAY, the TRUTH, and the LIFE..." Amen.

The silence has truly been broken, and our pulpits are coming alive with passionate preaching like never before. We are exchanging one-liners and old clichés for substance, signs, and wonders. People from all walks of life are coming to hear what "thus saith the Lord." Religion and God relationship are no longer to be referred to as an optional way of life, or as archaic, but rather our ONLY HOPE for the future! Hey, we've tried all their medications and social fixes. We've heard their trash talk on the radio. We have endured their presentations of propaganda; now it's our turn! I can almost hear it now: "This is My beloved Son, HEAR HIM!"

People are not satisfied with the current course of society. The silence has to be broken. Truth has been prisoner for too long. So preach on, preacher and pray on prayer warrior, because the silence of God has broken forth into some of the most powerful words that will ever be uttered or spoken. No one will have to ask where God is in our time; the world is going to know without doubt that He has chosen our generation through which to reveal Himself like never before.

Stay tuned, the truth is about to be proclaimed!!!

CHAPTER NINE

THE BEGINNING OF SORROWS

Generation X grew up in the "post-cold war era." We have had our fill of catastrophe preparation, public alert systems, and "worst-case scenario guides." Looking back now, it is so much clearer to see that our parents and those who had gone before us were simply trying to prepare us for the actual event (or as they say "an actual emergency"). They meant well; they were trying to keep us from being another statistic, I suppose.

We have learned much since those innocent days of preparation, but if one were to but casually glance into our times, they would see things that our parents never dreamed to prepare us for. We can look at these recent points of our history, however painful they may be, and extract a message that will help our generation endure the times to come...

The words of Jesus are as sobering as the sights that we have witnessed:

"And ye shall hear of wars and rumors of wars: see that ye be not troubled: for all these things must come to pass, but the end is not yet. For nation shall rise against nation, and kingdom against kingdom: and there shall be famines, and pestilences, and earthquakes, in strange places.

<u>All these are the beginning of sorrows</u>. Then shall they deliver you up to be afflicted, and shall kill you: and ye shall be hated of all nations for my name's sake.

And then shall many be offended, and shall betray one another, and shall hate one another. And many false prophets shall rise, and shall deceive many. And because iniquity shall abound, the love of many shall wax cold. But he that shall endure unto the end, the same shall be saved" (Matthew 24:6-13).

Nation against nation, kingdom against kingdom; famine, floods, fearful signs in the heavens and in the earth, and to beat all that, and a few earthquakes too! The Lord said that many would be tortured and betrayed, even by family and friends! Among the list and litany of hopelessness is an even more sobering message: "all these things are just the beginning of sorrows."

Yeah, that's what I thought too... Our parents never prepared us for this! It just doesn't get more realistic than this. To think that the things that our parents have witnessed and the things that we have witnessed in our short sum of days here on earth will pale in comparison to what will be seen in the days that lie ahead is a bit overwhelming to such a sheltered generation. Understand, this is not a doomsday prophecy, it is a reality check; there are some days of reckoning that yet belong to this generation, and I believe that God has allowed and will allow us to see some of these things, because we are the generation that has been chosen to declare His glory in the end time. The prophecy must ring true, "in the evening time there shall be light!" We of all generations need to be ready, because every word spoken from the beginning of time will more than likely find its end or prophetic fulfillment in our generation.

Ponder this for a moment; How else would an unbelieving world turn to us? How else can the "righteous shine forth as the sun," or there be "light in the evening time" except there is great darkness all about us? There is an ultimate day of awakening coming, and as we approach it, we need to be fearfully, reverently, respectfully, and soberly aware of it, and most of all... PREPARED!

The Word of God prepares us, saying that one day, "Every knee will bow, and every tongue will confess that Jesus Christ is Lord..."[2] To think of what must happen in the earth that would cause men and women of all ranks, classes, and societies to fall before God, whether in reverence or judgment, is beyond my being able to describe or even comprehend.

VIRTUAL REALITY

Our times are much more volatile than most are aware of. The headlines are violently boiling with new developments worldwide on the hour, every hour. God forbid that we would bury our head in the sand and expect somehow to escape the reality of all ages. Imagine if you will the terror that will fill the hearts of men on the ultimate day of reckoning. The airwaves will be filled with the voices of those who once refused to hear us, now saying, "God, please forgive us." The dealers will be trying to make deals, while the intellectuals will be trying to outsmart the system, but there will be none who will be left righteous by his own doing. There will be nowhere to run, nowhere to hide. No religious organization or affiliation, no help agency or firm. Our money will be worthless; our strength will be weak. Hopeless screams of terror will be silenced against a backdrop of countless opportunities denied.

No silver or gold, stocks or bonds, personalities or charisma will deter this day of virtual reality. Those who have called God all but good and have called on Him only when in selfish need will sorrow exceedingly. They have placed Him among all their other gods and taken His commandments from the public eye. They have destroyed the sanctity of human life; and so the saying will be true "who shall abide in that great day?" Hear it, "EVERY KNEE WILL BOW," the president, the moviemaker, the lawyer, the teacher, the preacher, the rock stars, the parents, and the children. Every knee, the good and the bad, the young and the old; all will bow and know that He is God. To some He will be Savior, to others Judge, but to all He will be the King of Kings and Lord of Lords.

We are but mere grains of dust when compared to eternity and the power of God, and yet at times, men have stood so boldly and ignorantly on their own in the face of God.

We need be reminded that we are but mortal men who dwell in days upon which God has appointed an end.

What a humbling and mortifying revelation... The rest is on the way.

CHAPTER TEN

WHO'S YOUR DADDY?

"...enter not into the fields of the fatherless" (Proverbs 23:10)

We have wandered in such fields for much too long in this generation. We have spent years without purpose and certain direction, victim to every "wind of doctrine, and sleight of men."[1] We are a generation whose umbilical cords of identity have been severed between us and our Source by the powers of the age. The enemy's plan was deadly: He knew that to disconnect the cords of relationship between father and child was to completely confuse and distort who we are supposed to be and how we are to operate as children of the Most High God. Jesus (the SON) had a source for His earthly being and ministry. He made reference to the importance of that source and maintaining connection continually.

Jesus said, when you pray, pray like this: "<u>Our Father</u> which is in Heaven..." Even when Jesus the Son Himself prayed, He tapped the source. "Jesus lifted up his eyes, and said, Father, I thank thee that thou hast heard me" (John 11:41).

As the Son of God, Jesus walked in constant communion with the Father of humanity, because He of all people knew the importance of this relationship. As sons of God, we too must make that same connection and realize how truly important that it is if we are to go forth and do the great things that the Father has prescribed us to do.

"As many as received HIM [as their Father], gave He POWER to become the sons of God..." (John 1:12). We must recognize this relationship if we are to have power in our time! The religious of Jesus's day said among themselves: "We have Abraham as our father." What they really meant was, "Our religion has worked just fine for us for thousands of years; don't try to change us now." The problem with their argument was that Abraham was dead and gone and they were not submitting themselves to anyone or connected to any source within their day! Their "Father" was religiosity! They would not receive God as their Father; therefore they were doing service to a man who was long dead and a law that they could not fulfill on their own. John the Baptist was right on when he answered this religious generation saying, **"I say unto you, that God is able of these stones to raise up children unto Abraham" (Matthew 3:9).**

The Words of Jesus at this point couldn't be any clearer, **"Call no man your father upon the earth: for one is your Father, which is in heaven" (Matthew 23:9).**

"IN HIM IS LIFE and this life is [truly] the light of men."[2] This is the true life source of our being. Once again, **"The Son can do nothing of himself, but what he sees the Father do" (John 5:19).** Jesus walked in constant affirmation and communion with the Father in order to accomplish His work in the earth. In John 8:16, we hear Him say, "I am not alone [or I am not working by myself as an earthly being], the Father sent [or empowered] me." (Additions mine). In John 8:18, He says, "the Father that sent Me bears witness of Me." One cannot be without the other, the Father empowers and constantly affirms the work of the Son... so who's your Daddy?

This relationship brings constant affirmation to the son; by this affirmation, he has power to operate according to the will of the Father. Remember, the seed of conception is in the Father (or the Spirit), without this (Spirit) seed there are no sons. (We'll talk more about this later.) There were occasions when the Son of God would operate that you would hear the voice of affirmation in the background saying, "This is My beloved Son in whom I am well pleased"[3] Again we hear Jesus (Our Father) saying to the sons of God in the New Testament that "these signs shall follow them that believe..." Notice this then, the Father's voice still confirms the sons of God today. The signs that follow believers are equal to the same voice of confirmation that Jesus the Son received from His Heavenly Father (or source) as He dwelt here on earth!

So many of our generation are wandering aimlessly, without hope or direction, simply because they have not made connection with their source; and because this connection is disrupted, there is no true affirmation, there are no true signs and wonders following. No affirmation, no signs, no wonders, no power... hell has severed the cords of the most important life source a true son could ever have.

Studies and statistics have proven again and again that if you remove the role of the father from the home and society, you have an instant imbalance so severe that the children will wander about confused and helpless unto their own destruction, despite alternate parental figures.[4] Children who lose connection with their parents lose their natural identity! (This is proven to be true both physically and spiritually.)

The argument of the religious in Jesus's day is much like the argument of those of our day. Everybody seems to be doing service to someone or something. The problem is not so much the service, however, but rather the loss of connection with the proper source.

"You do the deeds of your father. And they said to Him, we are not born illegitimately; we have one Father, even God. Jesus answered them and said, If God was your Father, you would love Me: for I proceeded forth and came from God as well; I did not come from Myself, But HE sent me [I know who My Daddy is].

But why do you not understand what I am saying? Because you cannot hear or understand My words, you have a different daddy, the devil, and so you are doing what your daddy would do. He was a murderer from

the beginning, and did not live in the truth, and there is no truth in him. When he speaks a lie, he speaks his own learned language, for he is a liar, and the father of lies" (John 8:41-44 additions mine).

So here is wisdom; we will do the deeds of our Daddy. What we hear of Him we speak, and what we see of Him we do. We cannot, as sons of God, boldly proclaim the gospel and power of Jesus Christ in our generation if we are not truly connected to Him as our life source. So... who is your Daddy?

CHAPTER ELEVEN

INSERT CHURCH HERE

We've talked about where we've been and how we've arrived at where we are now. We've talked about what we shouldn't be doing, so now let's talk about where we should be and what we should be doing. This should be no problem at all... We should be on our faces before God and men, humbling ourselves, repenting of the selfish error of our ways. That's where we should be.

"If My people which are called by My Name, shall humble themselves, and pray, and seek My face; and turn from their wicked ways; then will I hear from heaven, and will forgive their sin, and will heal their land" (2 Chronicles 7:14).

It just doesn't get any clearer than this.

There are two major levels on which repentance must take place before we can see apostolic revival in our time. The first level belongs to us, the people of God. God said, "If <u>MY PEOPLE</u>..." This is a direct reference to the people of God and no one else. Another writer says, **"the time is come that <u>judgment must begin at the house (or people) of God</u>..." (1 Peter 4:17).**

Jesus said to the church, "You are the light of the world, a city set upon a hill..." (Matthew 5:14). If we aren't shining, the world is in darkness for certain. If we cannot get it right, then there is no way the world will! It's time to "let God be true."[1]

Here's a harsh reality for some... We do not corner the market of the mind of God, and there are some things that will remain a secret in God until the time of His choosing. The wise man said, "the secret things belong to the Lord" (Deuteronomy 29:29) and for good reason: If He had handed it all to us, we would have made a great mess of it by now! He has given us the course to follow, the Spirit to lead, and the power to live "soberly and righteously in this present *age*."[2]

We do not need a new message or a new revelation. Jesus said, "THIS GOSPEL shall be preached in all the world for a witness..."[3] We need not look for another! Too many in our ranks and time have been confused by the multifaceted and yet static opinions of men. The progressive truth of God and His eternal identity is powerful and capable enough to endure and abide on its own accord. Like the flaming sword that turned every way that was placed at the gateway to the Garden of Eden,[4] the sword of God's Word needs none to uphold it, affirm it, or ratify its subject matter. God's thoughts are exactly that - God's thoughts. Scripture clearly reveals that God's thoughts and our thoughts are totally estranged and foreign to one another.

Now, although this truth is all-powerful in many aspects, it is noteworthy also to acknowledge its fragility. We need to note that the slightest changes have erred unto ultimate destruction. If Jesus says, "You must be," then you must be! (John 3:1-8). If God's Word says, "they shall," then THEY SHALL! (Mark 16:16-18). Let's leave these things and others like them exactly the way we found them! We have subjected the gospel of all times, to its worst enemy in our times... OPINION! This gospel that has survived countless fires, floods, and tyrants' rage is now at the mercy of the very ones who have held it near and dear for so long. It must begin with us.

FIRST THINGS FIRST

How should we ever expect to win a world entrenched in sin when we have it in our own hearts? God help us all! We have built our own boxes and kingdoms. We have closed ourselves off from the rest of the world, trying to convince ourselves, God, and everybody else that we are better off. Separation from worldliness is one thing; separation from reality and the world we have been commissioned to change is quite another.

"The time has come that judgment must begin at the house of God [or with the people of God]: and if it first begin at us, what shall the end of them that obey not the gospel of God." (1 Peter 4:17 KJV adaptations mine)

If we, the "body of Christ," fail miserably in our mission, then we can only assume that all those who have not heard of this wonderful truth will fall into the Hands of God, ignorant of their pending judgment, and yet they will not go alone. Their blood God will require at our hands.

We are the light of the world, a "city set upon a hill." In all of our bickering, floundering, and insecurity; in all of our contest and inactivity, still we shine, and the world looks on in dismay as we call ourselves the children of God. I suppose it needful to remind you now, that every great revival and awakening started with the church (everything good always does). We've got to get this right, and we've got to ask God to forgive us.

The second level of repentance belongs to the world around us. Repentance will swiftly move from the church to the outside world if we (the Church) will get in our place. In order for God to work as He has planned, men must be convinced of their evil deeds. As the church awakens, there will be a front of absoluteness that the world will have to recognize.

The prophet Isaiah says, "When YOUR judgments are in the earth, the inhabitants of the world will learn righteousness" (Isaiah 26:9).

That's correct, and you can mark it down, the day is upon us, and as the church takes action, all will see the true damage that has been done by allowing immorality and perversion of judgment to infiltrate our culture and society. It is at this point that many will turn to God in repentance. They need to hear the message:

"Be not deceived; God will not be mocked: whatever a man sows, that is what he will reap" (Galatians 6:7). The judgment of God against the sin of lawlessness and rebellion in our time will be openly manifest for all to see. It is time for those on the outside of the church walls to come to repentance and turn from their wicked ways before it is too late.

Somebody tell the world, "it's time to humble your pride, you need help and it is very apparent that your programs and social bandages alone are not getting the job done." You've taken prayer out of school[4] and it's time to put it back in. You've taken CHRIST out of Christmas, and THANKS out of Thanksgiving. It's time to get right from the White House to the local courthouse. We must go back and lay claim again to the morals and ideas of our true forefathers. All of the liberty and honor that men of valor in other generations and times so courageously fought for must be recaptured in our times and it will be if men and women everywhere will but humble their pride and repent.

WHO CAN CHANGE THE WORLD?

"With my soul have I desired thee in the night; yea, with my spirit within me will I seek thee early..." (Isaiah 26:9)

There are many times I wish I could write some wonderful new National Anthem or speak at the inauguration of the presidency, but just in case I do not last to seize the opportunity, I shall speak my peace now.

America has been so blessed; blessed because of her foundations, blessed because of her beginnings, blessed because of the faith of our forefathers. We of our generation are blessed in so many ways because of sacrifices made by men and women who traded their personal comforts and desires to pay the high cost of freedom. To these men and women, our prosperity is in constant debt. In the minds of these first pioneers, freedom had a whole different meaning than it does in our time.

As a nation, we need to remind ourselves that we have the prosperity and peace that we have because our forefathers chose to place themselves *"UNDER GOD."* There are countless examples of nations and kingdoms that have refused to place themselves under His divine hand, and they have quickly come to ruin. Just a thought, but worthy of entertaining is the fact that more inventions and modern conveniences have been birthed in our country (or at least because of our aid) than anywhere else in the modern world; and why, because we are so smart? No, we are blessed! Every country in the world has partaken of the blessing that is upon us in one way or another.

Finally, and more individually, we are blessed as a people of God. There are so many things that our presence in the local community and world has kept the world at large from experiencing because of who we are and what we stand for. Think about it: God would not destroy Sodom because of Abraham's family connection and intercession.[5] We need to recognize this blessing, as well as our part in its continuance in us as individuals. We may not completely change the times in which we live to the degree that we desire, but we can certainly provide a witness for the world to see where this "true light that lights every man" comes from. Let freedom ring, let freedom reign, and let truth be known, possessed, and proclaimed from sea to shining sea. We must all see our part in the turning of a whole nation and generation to repentance toward God so that His true glory can be revealed.

CHAPTER TWELVE

THE SONS OF GOD

"I consider that the sufferings of this present time are not worth comparing with the glory that is to be revealed to us. For the creation waits with eager longing <u>for the revealing of the sons of God</u>; for the creation was subjected to futility, not of its own will but by the will of him who subjected it in hope; because the creation itself will be set free from its bondage to decay and obtain the glorious liberty of the children of God." (Romans 8:18-21 RSV)

There is a mysterious shaking within the earth these days; the long-awaited appearance of the Sons of God on the scene of humanity, operating in full apostolic authority, as designed by God Himself. Oh the "glorious liberty of the children of God."[1] Oh what power is given them in the earth for such a time as this; If only our eyes were opened and we could see the things that are freely given of God and that belong to us as His children... the earth groans to see their appearing. And why wouldn't all creation groan, awaiting their manifestation? If by the disobedience of the first Adam, the earth was placed under bondage, then by the obedience and restoration of the second (or the last) it would be released from such decay![2]

"Beloved, <u>NOW</u> are we the sons of God, and it doth not yet appear what we shall be: but we know that, when he shall appear, we shall be like him; for we shall see him as he is." (1 John 3:2 KJV)

Though it "does not yet appear what we shall be," we need not withhold our operation. We "are the sons of God" **NOW**. We may not always feel like it, or look like it, but our "present condition," as the apostle Paul said, is not even worthy to be compared with the glory that will be revealed in us. We cannot afford to withhold our identity any longer. Not only are we taught by God's Word how to live and walk in this present generation, but we are also commanded to walk in power, authority, and victory, conquering our every waking moment as sons of God.

"NOW" is the only moment in history that we possess the power to affect or alter!

If we do not conquer the time in which we live, then all the truth that we have preached and all the things that we have done to promote it within this time will become prisoner to ages gone by. I don't know about you, my friend, but I do not want my generation to be just another bedtime story. Necessity, my friend, is upon the "NOW"!

The call to sonship and apostolic operation is long overdue. We have allowed ourselves to exist far too long, living far below our potential. When we look at the ministry of Jesus Christ here on earth as the Son of God, it doesn't take long at all for the student of the Word to notice the zeal and urgency that He walked in, a zeal and desperation activated by the understanding of the office in which He dwelt. Jesus not only understood His location, but also His duration. He knew that his office as an earthly Son was a temporary one and the zeal for that office literally "ate Him up"[3]!

Jesus knew who He was, how He was, and how long He had to walk as the "Son of God." To those who received Him, He "gave power to become sons"[4] as well; Thus with this power, we must "walk as He walked"[5] - in urgency and operation.

"BELOVED NOW..." Not later, not maybe, NOW! We are the most valuable asset in God's Kingdom today because we can affect the "now." Those who have gone on before us can do nothing more. Those who belong to the future can do nothing yet. But being a son of God is all about living and doing in the here and now. We hear from certain "sons" of the gospel speaking out to encourage future generations. Notice the urgency that typically accompanies their message.

Solomon, the son of David, said, "Remember <u>NOW</u> thy creator in the days of your youth" (Ecclesiastes 12:1). The prophet Haggai said to the Lord, "<u>Speak NOW</u>..." Jesus the SON told John the Baptist on the river of His coronation, "Suffer it to be so <u>NOW</u>..." Notice the words of the Apostle Peter when he says, "The times of our ignorance God winked at, but <u>NOW</u> commands that all men everywhere repent!" (Acts 17:30).

The writer of the book of Hebrews says, "<u>NOW faith</u>,"[6] this is the kind of faith that can change a present world. Abraham believed in his day, Paul believed in his, and now it's up to us to believe in ours!!!! Jesus Christ the Son walked in the urgency of the office saying, **"I MUST do the works which I was sent to do while it is day..." (John 9:4).** We as sons and daughters of that same Son should walk in the same urgency and motivation.

The shadow of my finger cast
Divides the future from the past;
Before it stands the unborn hour
  In darkness and beyond thy power;
Behind its un-returning line
The vanished hour, no longer thine;
  One hour alone is in thy hands,
  The NOW on which the shadow stands.
      Henry Van Dyke (1904)

SONS IN DANGER

The enemy of our soul hates the office and operation of sonship, for it is this same office that dwells in the same earthly realm in which the he himself was cast. Son-ship is the devil's constant adversary and contender. When the "Word became flesh"[7] one can notice that the first thing the enemy did was to try to get the world and even the Son of God Himself to question His identity. The temptation in the wilderness reveals this in clarity.

"Then was Jesus led up of the Spirit into the wilderness to be tempted of the devil. And when he had fasted forty days and forty nights, he was afterward hungery. And when the tempter came to him, he said, If thou be the Son of God, command that these stones be made bread. But he answered and said, it is written,

Man shall not live by bread alone, but by every word that proceedeth out of the mouth of God. Then the devil taketh him up into the holy city, and setteth him on a pinnacle of the temple, And saith unto him, If thou be the Son of God, cast thyself down: for it is written, He shall give his angels charge concerning thee: and in their hands they shall bear thee up, lest at any time thou dash thy foot against a stone. Jesus said unto him, it is written again, Thou shalt not tempt the Lord thy God.

Again, the devil taketh him up into an exceeding high mountain, and sheweth him all the kingdoms of the world, and the glory of them; And saith unto him, All these things will I give thee, if thou wilt fall down and worship me. Then saith Jesus unto him, get thee hence, Satan: for it is written, Thou shalt worship the Lord thy God, and him only shalt thou serve." **(Matthew 4:1-10)**

The enemy has tried to confuse and frustrate the identity of the sons of God in our time, much the same as he did the Son of God from the beginning. The Scripture reveals that the "god of this world has blinded the minds"[8] of potential sons and daughters of God in an effort to completely confuse and destroy the work of God through them in our day. hell trembles at the very thought of the fact that we as heirs to the throne of God have power "over all of the power of the enemy."[9] For this reason, satan constantly bombards our minds and hearts, endeavoring to sever the most important cords of relationship and understanding that we will ever have as children. As long as a people walk in ignorance of who they are, they are powerless to operate according to the power of the Son of God.

Though John said, "it does not yet appear..." we must understand that we have the power of God as sons through birth and by faith! No matter what the enemy may do to confuse this, we must daily declare unto ourselves, "I am presently a rightful heir by virtue of the fact that I have been born into the family of God!!! I am not an intruder or an outsider but I have been birthed into this family and have access as a rightful heir to all that pertains to my Father's throne."

The Apostle John kindly reminds us that "We are of God, [If it be so that we are born into His Kingdom] and have overcome them: Because GREATER is He that is in us, than he that is in the world" (1 John 4:4).

CHAPTER THIRTEEN

THE ULTIMATE GENERATION

Jesus says of this generation, "nothing shall be impossible to you" (Matt. 17:20). This is Kingdom authority that transcends all authority of its time. "NO WEAPON FORMED AGAINST IT WILL PROSPER!"

Not only did God "predestine" the church before the world began, but He also allowed men at certain times to look into many of the things that He had planned and predestined to be a part of its unfolding and revealing. John the revelator looks beyond the veil of time and space and writes the following to define what we will call "the ultimate generation."

"And after these things I saw <u>ANOTHER ANGEL</u> come down from heaven, having great power; and the earth was lightened with his glory"   (Revelation 18:1).

Notice that I have highlighted the fact that John sees "another angel." His reference to this angel as "another" seems to point to his attempt to describe an angel that was quite different than all others he had seen before it. This is "another" and not the same as others by virtue of God's choosing and highlighting it to reveal something that would otherwise be hidden to man. God is drawing John's attention to this angel, just as God is drawing attention to this generation and the days we are now living in. What this particular angel possesses causes it to stand out against the background of the time it was revealed in.

"Ye are a chosen generation, a royal priesthood, an holy nation, a peculiar people; that ye should shew

forth the praises of him who hath called you out of darkness into his marvelous light" (1 Peter 2:9).

The angel John is describing seems to be a different kind of angel than those he witnessed carrying the vials, or blowing the trumpets. This angel seems to refer to the type of angels that were spoken of in Revelation 2 and 3, which represent a group of people in a particular place, time, or generation... the "angels of the church."

Notice that John records specifically that this particular angel's origin was from heaven. At first thought, we must ask ourselves, well "aren't all angels from heaven?" But John notes more specifically that it wasn't just the fact that this angel was from heaven, but more specifically the power and ability of its operation in the earth was from heaven. In other words, the angel's power did not come from the present world (or age) with all of its intellectual resources, but this angel was operating on power from another dimension, power from above. This helps in further defining WHO this angel really represents. The Apostle James wrote that every good and perfect gift "comes from above" (James 1:17). Again, we read in the book of Acts (the origin of the church) and find that what we possess as a people came "**FROM HEAVEN.**" We're on to something here...

"And when the day of Pentecost was fully come, they were all with one accord in one place. And suddenly there came a sound from heaven as of a rushing mighty wind, and it filled all the house where they were sitting" (Acts 2:1,2).

Jesus Christ - the initiator and founder of this great experience and generation said to those of His day, "I am from above...I am not of this world" (John 8:23). There were those of His day that could trace the source of their foundations or experience back to some council, board meeting, or humanly engineered or governed experience, just as there are many groups and denominations of our time that could do the same. In Paul's day, there were those who said, "What we have comes from John the Baptist." (Acts 19) In Jesus's day, they said, "What we have comes from Abraham." But I am glad to tell you that as a first partaker of the regenerate power of the Holy Ghost, that what we have comes from HEAVEN!

Not only is this angel's point of origin from another world, but it was recognized by John as having "great power." This angel (or generation) is seen as having "great power" because it is recognized as power, not of its own accord, but it is significant of Divine power and supernatural authority. Evidently, this angel has been entrusted with this great power. This is the same power spoken of in Matthew 28:18 when Jesus said, "ALL POWER IS GIVEN UNTO ME IN HEAVEN AND IN EARTH." Again we hear Jesus say to His disciples, **"Behold, I give unto you power to tread on serpents and scorpions, and over all the power of the enemy: and nothing shall by any means hurt you. Notwithstanding in this rejoice not, that the spirits are subject unto you; but rather rejoice, because your names are written in heaven" (Luke 10:19, 20).**

Notice that He says don't rejoice that you have this power, but rather rejoice that your origin and destination is not of this world! He gave us power not to tread here alone, but to live free from this world, and to liberate others as well.

"...having GREAT POWER..."

Here we are again, **"Ye shall receive power, after that the Holy Ghost is come upon you: and ye shall be witnesses unto me both in Jerusalem, and in all Judea, and in Samaria, and unto the uttermost part of the earth" (Acts 1:8).**

This "power" is not only described as the power to accomplish, but it is simultaneously and more effectively described as the power to "know," understand, or unlock previously guarded information. This power is the unction from the Holy One that John said causes us to "know all things."[1] This is a direct fulfillment of the "Spirit of Truth" that Jesus said would come upon us and would teach us all things. Now that's power! When Jesus handed Peter the keys to the Kingdom, He gave him that power. This was not only power to accomplish, but power to open doors of understanding and authority like never before!

Jesus says to this generation, "Nothing shall be impossible to you" (Matt. 17:20). This is Kingdom authority that transcends all authority of its time. It can be declared to this generation unequivocally, "NO WEAPON FORMED AGAINST IT WILL PROSPER!"[2]

John then records not only the immediate difference in appearance of the angel, and not only the origin and power with which it operated, but also that the whole earth was "lightened" or illuminated by the glory that shone from it. The whole earth was lightened, or we could say, "the whole world was illuminated" or brought to understanding by the light that shone from this great gospel. Interestingly enough this is the identical illumination that the Apostle Paul was referring to when he said, **"...the eyes of your understanding being enlightened (or illuminated); that you may know..." (Ephesians 1:18).**

The purpose of this light is to bring understanding to all the residents of the earth in a time of perilous darkness. This would be a direct fulfillment of the prophecy spoken by Zechariah when he said, **"...it shall come to pass, that at evening time it shall be light (illumination or understanding)" (Zechariah 14:7).** AMEN! The Greek word used here is *photidzo*, meaning understanding or illumination.

This light has a purpose; it is significant of revelatory understanding. The Apostle Paul says, **"God who commanded the light to shine out of darkness, has shined in our hearts giving us the light of the knowledge [or understanding] of the glory of God in the face of Jesus Christ" (2 Corinthians 4:6).** This is the light of the revelation of JESUS CHRIST!

This light has a source: The source could not be simpler than that of the "Father of lights,"[3] that "true light that gives light to every man that comes into the world"[4] in whom was life **"and this life was the LIGHT of men, this light shines in darkness and the darkness cannot comprehend it [or those who are in darkness cannot understand, therefore His light brings them understanding]" (John 1:4, 5).**

Again, "They looked unto Him (the light source) and were lightened (or enlightened)" (Psalms 34:5).

David Bryan

This light is a people: **"You are the light of the world. A city that is set on a hill cannot be hid" (Matthew 5:14).**

"The whole earth was lightened..." Think about that the next time you consider your light and influence to be small and insignificant! This is an absolute parallel to the prophecy of Daniel when he said, **"They that be wise (or enlightened) shall shine as the brightness of the firmament; and they that turn many to righteousness as the stars forever and ever" (Daniel 12:3).** We need to understand just how powerful this generation really is: Jesus says to this generation, "Blessed are your eyes for they see and your ears for they do hear and you understand" (Matthew 13:16). We have been "illuminated" by the Spirit of God!

There is great merit to the fact that God instructed Daniel to, "...shut up the words, and seal the book, even to the time of the end" (Daniel 12:4). Because God knew that then and only then would there dwell a generation who would actually know what to do with the words that were spoken.

THE VOICE OF A NEW GENERATION

One final detail concerning this generation... The Bible says that this "angel" "cried mightily with a strong voice." It is a voice of warning, a voice of revelation and understanding; a voice of great and notable authority.

In other times, when John heard an angel speaking or calling out, he records that the voice was "loud" or "great" but this is the one occasion in which we hear him describe an angel's voice as being "STRONG." "Loud" is of volume, and "great" is of stature or authority, but "strong" is of proven and gathered experience. In other words, this voice had gained its power and strength through time and tribulation. This voice is not the voice of one individual, but rather many individuals whose personal understandings and situations gathered and matured over time to become proven truth. This voice is sweetened with age and proven through experience. This voice is loud even when spoken softly, and it is great even when

74

spoken by the weakest who believe it. It's not the voice so much, but rather the content of the message!

This voice began its journey through such stuttering men as Moses saying, "Who is on the Lord's side?"[5] And again at the foot of the mount saying, "Hear O Israel!"[6] Joshua felt the force of its message as the Word befell him, and said, "As for me and my house, we will serve the Lord!"[7] We hear the voice continue to strengthen as it passes through the story of Esther and we hear her say, "If I perish, then I perish, but I will see the king!"[8] And of course, who can forget little David out in the field with the giant saying, "I come to you in the Name of the Lord of Hosts."[9]

It is the voice of the prophet Elijah in the valley with the prophets of baal saying, "Make up your minds, gentlemen, which god are you going to serve?"[10] It is the voice of one "crying in the wilderness, preparing the way of the Lord."[11] This voice had gained such intensity that by the time it fell to John the Baptist, thousands went out to hear him. And finally, it was a strong voice that declared a whole new generation on the hill of Golgotha when Jesus cried, "IT IS FINISHED,"[12] When this voice was released in agony the rocks and the mountains trembled with fear, knowing this voice was not like any other.

This message was not strong because of the men who spoke it, because quite frankly, most of them were weak. Again, the voice is not strong because of the volume that men may or may not have spoken it with. But this voice is strong because of the enduring and proven content of its message. This great voice resounded on the day of Pentecost as the apostle stood to proclaim the greatest message of all time, **"Repent and be baptized everyone of you in the Name of Jesus Christ for the remission of sins, and you shall receive the gift of the Holy Ghost" (Acts 2:38).** I am glad to report that this voice and this message are stronger now than ever. Listen, folks, we need not fear for the content, let's just open our mouths and speak and tell it like it is!

Jesus told Peter, "Don't worry about what you will say, I will give you a mouth to speak with..."[13] and He did! If we would trust God, He would speak the same message in our time and we would see many turned to righteousness. REMEMBER, it's not so much the speaker, it's the content of the message that gets the job done... There is one more voice that cries after this angel, and it is the voice of the Lord. As we stand to be revealed as the "angel" of this generation, God will punctuate the words of our mouth with His mighty power! And what is the message that follows the revelation of this ultimate generation of people; but a message of separation and true holiness unto the Lord. Look closely, my friend, for an ultimate generation has been birthed before our very eyes.

CHAPTER FOURTEEN

IT'S OUR TURN!

Jesus was speaking to His disciples concerning a time that was totally foreign to their understanding, a time that better fits our here and now. He described to them a time when nation would rise against nation, and kingdom against kingdom. "Earthquakes in strange places, famines, sickness, and fearful sights..."

Jesus warned his disciples that those who proclaimed this message would be persecuted and delivered into prison, "for My Name's sake" (Luke 21:10-12). But then He says something at the close of His discourse that ought to cause us to take a much closer look: **"It shall turn to you for a testimony" (Luke 21:13).** In other words, all of these things that are prophesied to happen will allow an opportunity of ministry and witness into a time that needs a witness the most.

Jesus was preparing His chosen for the time when all of humanity would turn in our direction, and all eyes would be upon us. It is at this time that God will require that we do something with what we possess, "give an answer of the hope that lies within us"[1] if you please. As we look at the headlines of our day and the intensity with which things are taking place, it appears to be a divine setup. I am convinced that events such as the ones that have befallen our times are permitted of God, not only to take the high and mighty out of their dream world into reality, but to provide an opportunity for His children to shine forth! "It's OUR TURN!"

Look at the following Scripture the way that the NIV describes this scenario, **"They will lay hands on you and persecute you. They will deliver you to synagogues and prisons, and you will be brought before kings and governors, and all because of My Name. This will result in your**

being a witness unto them. But make up your mind and do not worry beforehand how you will defend yourselves. For I will give you words and wisdom that none of your adversaries will be able to resist or contradict" (Luke 21:12-19).

Again verse 13 is our focus, saying, "It shall turn to you for a testimony," or as the NAS says, "it will lead into an opportunity for (the world to hear) your testimony." This was God's way of letting us know by virtue of His Word and the unfolding of His will that we will have our turn to declare His greatness. All along, God has been preparing us for the day when all other voices would fall silent, and ours would be clearly heard, and that day is nigh upon us!

We have stood in the background for far too long; we've learned all too well how to tread carefully among the careless. The world has heard from Constantine, Tertullian, St. Augustine, Pope Gregory, John Calvin, Martin Luther, John Wesley, and a plethora of other popular reformists and theological icons of years gone by. Many people have sold out their own potential to follow in the shadows of such men and have become nothing more than traditionalists and philosophers themselves, mere marionettes of religiosity. Who are these to define our day? No matter how great they were in their time, I for one refuse to allow them to define a generation and an experience that many of these men had not even personally witnessed! Who are they to say that there are not higher heights and deeper depths to God's ultimate design?

I'm not interested in how many books great men may have written, or how popular they were or are. People are hungry for more than just good "wordage" and flashy sermonizing. God is stirring the hearts of men in the midst of perilous times. To think of it, most of the words that the traditional religious world has adhered so dogmatically to have faded away into utter uselessness against the times that are now upon us; so what does that say about the depth of their theology? It's time for a fresh voice, the voice of a new generation; "It's OUR TURN!"

I am not discrediting the fact that God has indeed used many men of past generations and even of our time to provoke us onward into greater light and understanding, I am also not saying that God hasn't employed mules to speak on His behalf either, because the fact of the matter is, He has!. We must remember, however, that these men's thoughts and words were merely a means to an end, and NOT the end of the matter within themselves. God gave these men such understanding to highlight what He had already spoken from the beginning, not alter or change it, and that's where many have gone astray. God's will and plan is progressive, and there remain yet days to be defined and prophecies to be fulfilled.

These men were but tools, preparing the world for a time to come when the gospel would fill the airwaves and the hearts of men; a time when the Spirit of God would be poured out in unprecedented measure. That time is NOW, and "It's our turn!" We need not fear what we will say or do; God has promised and already proven that if we will set ourselves into position and open our mouths, that He will fill our mouths with His wisdom and power!

Jesus told us that we would "reap where we have not sown,"[2] and "enter into other men's labors." We are not entering as intruders, but as guests unto the completion of the work that was begun at Calvary. Those who have gone before us have simply loosened the lid on the proverbial jar, but now that it has turned to us, with ease we have opened into a whole new world of power, operation, and understanding.

HE SAVED THE BEST FOR LAST

And why wouldn't He? It's just like God to reserve the best for the last so that He could end this thing with a bang. Eschatologically [if I may so use the word in such a way]speaking, there is evidence within the Word of God of a great ingathering of an end-time generation that will operate in unparalleled anointing in the closing moments of human history. The words that God instructed former prophets to seal were the words and instructions that have been reserved and belong to a time and a people of God's choosing. Isn't it great to know that God has saved the best for last!

"Though thy beginning was [seemed] small, yet thy latter end should greatly increase" Job 8:7.

Why the increase in the latter end? Because God saves the best for last! In the evening time, at the end "there shall be light!"

"He that endures unto the end shall be saved" (Matthew 10:22). So why is the end better than the beginning? Because that which remains unto the end has been tried unto maturity, strengthened through process; it will stand the test of the times - it can be trusted! We do not simply belong to the age, but this age belongs to us; it's our time to shine! There is an anointing which God has reserved for these last times that will confound the wisest among us. The prophet declares, "The glory of the latter house shall be greater than that of the former."[3] Why? Because God saved the best for the last!

The Scripture reveals that God would call a people, who were "not a people."[4] In other words, they were not previously recognized to be a part of what many thought would be the proverbial "church scene." God has reached beyond the boundaries of the typical and the known into the unknown. According to the prophet Joel, there are some "mighty ones"[5] among the commoners of our day who were seemingly useless and unnamed just a few short years ago. These are now understood to be that which God has ordained to complete His work in the earth! Truly, He saved the best for last! If God would have placed us anywhere else in time, we would have had to be content with the mediocrity of it; but be it known this day that He has saved the best for last!

It may have appeared in recent years that those who have stood for the morals and principles of Truth have become obsolete and archaic, but God has reserved this generation all long. Let me remind the reader that it was the so-called "evangelical Christian" vote here in America that turned the tides in our most recent presidential election. (It wasn't necessarily the man that mattered as much as the issues on the ballots, that's what we really voted for.) This should be our cue, it's time to move; God has empowered our voice!

These whom God has reserved unto the last are the employed and the empowered, the anointed of God. The likes of which the prophet Joel said, "...there have never been or will be hereafter." This is the greatest time ever to be alive, and we must heed the voice of God that is prompting us to move onto the scene, because it's our turn! **CODE ADAM**

We are the empowered and the unstoppable. We will run through troops, Raise up the dead, tear down the strongholds of the enemy, and leap over the walls of opposition. God has anointed us to preach and pray with such conviction and power that even the greatest of earthly intelligence cannot comprehend or withstand the power that shall prevail.

"Strengthen ye the weak hands, and confirm the feeble knees. Say to them that are of a fearful heart, Be strong, fear not: behold, your God will come with vengeance, even God with a recompense; he will come and save you.

Then the eyes of the blind shall be opened, and the ears of the deaf shall be unstopped. Then shall the lame man leap as an hart, and the tongue of the dumb sing: for in the wilderness shall waters break out, and streams in the desert. And the parched ground shall become a pool, and the thirsty land springs of water: in the habitation of dragons, where each lay, shall be grass with reeds and rushes. And a highway shall be there, and a way and it shall be called The way of holiness; the unclean shall not pass over it; but it shall be for those: the wayfaring men, though fools, shall not err therein. No lion shall be there, or any ravenous beast shall go up thereon, it shall not be found there; but the redeemed shall walk there: And the ransomed of the LORD shall return, and come to Zion with songs and everlasting joy upon their heads: they shall obtain joy and gladness, and sorrow and sighing shall flee away" (Isaiah 35:3-10).

Look at the Apostle Paul's description here of this great spiritual generation: **"There is a natural body, and there is a spiritual body. And so it is written; the first man Adam was made a living soul; the last Adam was made a quickening spirit. Howbeit that was not first which is spiritual, but that which is natural; and afterward that which is spiritual. [Notice here that He saved the best for last!]**

The first man is of the earth, earthy: the second man is the Lord from heaven. As is the earthy, such are they also that are earthy: and as is the heavenly, such are they also that are heavenly. And as we have borne the image of the earthy, we shall also bear the image of the heavenly" (1 Corinthians 15:44-49).

The last Adam (or generation) is given the pre-eminence; he is a "quickening spirit," empowered with the anointing of God Himself. He is a spiritual being capable of things which the first is unable. He truly has saved the best for last!

"Thus saith the LORD; Refrain thy voice from weeping, and thine eyes from tears: for thy work shall be rewarded, saith the LORD; and they shall come again from the land of the enemy. And there is hope in thine end, saith the LORD that thy children shall come again to their own border" (Jeremiah 31:16-20).

"Thy children shall come again to their own border." This is not only a prophecy of the return of the captivity of Israel, and the ingathering of the nation, but its spiritual parallel is of equal or greater significance. This is also a picture of a generation past and a church that once operated in apostolic authority coming again to their own border doing the "first works."[6] Peter, James, and John, they had their time, but now it's our turn!

"...your latter end will greatly increase." (Job 8:7)

It has appeared that we have with ease just taken the top off from things that have been difficult to access for so many generations. What we know to be true is that God saved a people for this time. The prophecy of Daniel says, **"...the people that do know their God shall be strong, and do exploits..."** (Daniel 11:32).

This is a picture of a relationship that is deeper than the typical surface relationships of our day. When Daniel describes those who "know" God, he means intimately. This is a relationship like none other; the kind of relationship and connection that is sure to bring forth fruit, power, signs, and wonders! These are they who have been born again and are in constant communion and operation with the Most High. We are the righteous that will **"shine forth as the sun in the Kingdom of Our Father"** (Matthew 13:43). Truly He has saved the best for last!

CHAPTER FIFTEEN

A FINAL WORD

"We are the only hope that tomorrow has, and when all that our forefathers have fought for ceases to be that which we are founded upon, it is time for an urgent awakening and that awakening belongs to us." – D. Bryan

If God should look into this generation as He has in other times, and find "none to help," woe will be unto us for certain. When the strongest among us are but weak spiritual replicas of days gone by, it is definitely time to sound the alarm. **CODE ADAM!**

Who we are as a people matters now more than ever before, we do not need a reasonable facsimile of the first church. We are however, in desperate need of a continuation of the things that defined us from the beginning. This is not the time to find ways to disguise the message God has entrusted to us, but rather to unveil it in its entirety. We are the missing link! We are the only hope that tomorrow has, and when all that our forefathers have fought for ceases to be that which we are founded upon, it is time for an urgent awakening.

"CODE ADAM" is that awakening. It's time to regroup, refocus, and re-establish ourselves in the earth. We cannot and we must not turn now from what lies before us. The neo-religious world would love for us to do so, because they know as long as we mount the pulpits of our time, they are forced to reckon with the lies and double standards they are so accustomed to propagating and living under.

We are the "light of the world." We are the very force that withholds the powers of darkness from being able to prevail in the earth at this very moment. We are the Church of the Living God, and if we should keep silent or allow ourselves to be distracted, it would be as if the earth were thrown off from its axis, or the stars tumbled from Heaven; it just cannot be! To think that our witness and actions coupled with the Spirit of God are the very forces that keep back the powers of darkness from filling the earth is more than sobering, it is utterly inspirational.

So stand now, Adam, wherever you are; stand and be accounted for. Give yourself to service in God's Kingdom while there is time. The life that God has granted us is too short to do anything other than simply obey the call. The world is our stadium, the spotlights are the lamps of witness burning from all who have shone in ages past. It's our time to make a difference, to change our world, and we've got the power to do so. Adam whoever you are, wherever you are we need you now!

ENDNOTES

INTRODUCTION ENDNOTES

1.   On April 30, 2003, "**CODE ADAM** Act of 2003" became law. It requires that the designated authority for a public building establish procedures for a child missing in a federal facility. On November 1, 2003, the Department of Homeland Security Federal Protective Service (FPS) implemented a policy nationwide establishing procedures for locating a missing child in federal facilities.

2.   **CODE ADAM** was established by the Wal-Mart retail chain... Information and Instructions and additional information are available through: NCMEC *(www.ncmec.org)*

CHAPTER 1 ENDNOTES

1.   Isaiah 21:11 (KJV)
2.   Revelation 3:17 is a direct reference to the church of Laodicea; the Laodicean people in ancient times were a prideful, idolatrous, self-indulgent, and self-sufficient people to whom God pronounced rebuke. The reference to this church is a parallel reference to the age in which we live. The similarities are uncanny.

CHAPTER 2 ENDNOTES

1.   In 1 Corinthians 14:7, the Apostle Paul draws reference to what he defines as "distinction in the sounds." Though he is using these "sounds" in reference to the operation of the gift of tongues, the parallel application is that of distinct or certain sounds of life that acquaint us with the familiar.
2.   Washington DC's thirtieth annual gay pride parade was held Saturday evening, June 11, 2005. (*Joe Tresh's Washington Saturday, June 25, 2005*)

3.   "Waco, Texas: Where a part of America's Heart and Soul died." By Robert McCurry (www.islandone.org).

4.   Oklahoma City Tragedy- CNN (www.cnn.com)

CHAPTER 3 ENDNOTES

1.   2 Kings 2:9-14.

2.   Rev. Jessie Williams /Ohio District UPCI Spring Conference, May 2004.

CHAPTER 5 ENDNOTES

1.   Grover Cleveland- The second inaugural address of Grover Cleveland Saturday, March 4, 1893 (The Avalon Project at Yale Law School: Documents in Law, History and Diplomacy. http://www.yale.edu/lawweb/avalon/avalon.htm.)

2.   Col 1:12-15 — "Giving thanks unto the Father, which hath made us meet to be partakers of the inheritance of the saints in light: Who hath delivered us from the power of darkness, and hath translated us into the kingdom of his dear Son: In whom we have redemption through his blood, even the forgiveness of sins: Who is the image of the invisible God, the firstborn of every creature" -KJV

CHAPTER 7 ENDNOTES

1.   Edmund Burke — This quotation most often attributed to Burke ("The only thing necessary for the triumph of evil is for good men to do nothing", along with many other variants and adaptations) are supposedly not his original writings. This particular quote may have been adapted from these lines of Burke's in his Thoughts on the Cause of Present Discontents (1770):"When bad men combine, the good must associate; else they will fall one by one, an un-pitied sacrifice in a contemptible struggle." The quotation is similar in sentiment and content to a quotation of John Philpot Curran (1750 - 1817), ascribed to a Speech on the Right of Election of Lord Mayor of Dublin, 10 July 1790: "The

condition upon which God hath given liberty to man is eternal vigilance; which condition, if he break, servitude is at once the consequence of his crime, and the punishment of his guilt."

2.   John Donne Meditation #17: "No man is an island..." (http://isu.indstate.edu/ilnprof/ENG451/ISLAND)

3.   Dennis Waitley (Teams and Teamwork/ Copyright © 2005 *QuotationsBook.com*)

CHAPTER 8 ENDNOTES

1.   Luke 19:37-40 records the Lord's triumphal entry into Jerusalem.

CHAPTER 9 ENDNOTES

1.   Zechariah 14:7.
2.   Philippians 2:11.

CHAPTER 10 ENDNOTES

1.   Ephesians 4:14.
2.   John 1:4.
3.   Matthew 3:17 records the voice of the Father speaking over the Son as He submitted Himself to the waters of Baptism in Jordan. Again we hear the voice of confirmation speaking in Matthew 17:5 on the mount of transfiguration.
4.   The Fatherless home syndrome/ Statistics on Fatherless America
(http://www.photius.com/feminocracy/facts on fatherless kids.html)

CHAPTER 11 ENDNOTES

1.   Romans 3:4 (KJV).
2.   Titus 2:12 (NKJV).
3.   Matthew 24:14 (KJV).

4. Genesis 3:24 (KJV) Notice also that even the Cherubim that were placed there had no handle on the Sword signifying God's ability to operate independent of all.
5. Genesis 18:23-31.

CHAPTER 12 ENDNOTES

1. Romans 8:21 (KJV).
2. 1 Corinthians 15:45-47 (KJV) ...it is written, The first man Adam was made a living soul; the last Adam was made a quickening spirit. Howbeit that was not first which is spiritual, but that which is natural; and afterward that which is spiritual. The first man is of the earth, earthy: the second man is the Lord from heaven. The "first man" was a man of sin, the "last man" or the 'second' is "the Lord." Jesus Christ became sin "though He knew no sin," to destroy the curse placed upon sinful humanity. After the birth of the spiritual man, the curse of sin is broken, thus when we reign as "kings and priests" with Christ, the earth also will be released from the power of the curse of sin.
3. John 2:17 (KJV).
4. John 1:12 (KJV).
5. 1 John 2:6 (KJV).
6. Hebrews 11:1 (KJV).
7. John 1:14 (KJV).
8. 2 Corinthians 4:4 (KJV).
9. Luke 10:19 (KJV).

CHAPTER 13 ENDNOTES

1. 1 John 2:20 (KJV).
2. Isaiah 54:17 (KJV).
3. James 1:17 (KJV).
4. John 1:9 (KJV).
5. Exodus 32:26 (KJV).
6. Deuteronomy 6:4 (KJV).
7. Joshua 24:15 (KJV).
8. Esther 4:16 (KJV).
9. 1 Samuel 17:45 (KJV).

10.   1 Kings 18:21 (KJV).
11.   Isaiah 40:3 (KJV).
12.   John 19:30 (KJV).
13.   Luke 21:15 (KJV).

CHAPTER 14 ENDNOTES

1.   1 Peter 3:15 (KJV).
2.   John 4:38 (KJV).
3.   Haggai 2:9 (KJV).
4.   1 Peter 2:10 (KJV).
5.   In Joel 3:9 The Lord says, "wake up the mighty men... let the weak say I am strong and the men of war draw near." The underlying understanding here is the fact that God is using this "unmarked people" to provoke His chosen people. Earlier in his prophecy, Joel says, "there has never been a people like this, neither shall there be again." This is the "chosen generation."
6.   Revelation 2:5 (KJV).

For information contact

Rev David Bryan
3805 Mount Vernon Blvd
Norton, Ohio 44203

Email: db@btown.cc

(330)745-5550 ext 201

For new and upcoming product information
Visit our store on the web @

www.dbevangelist.com